FRANCE AND SHERWOOD ANDERSON

SHERWOOD ANDERSON

FRANCE AND SHERWOOD ANDERSON: PARIS NOTEBOOK, 1921

Michael Fanning

LOUISIANA STATE UNIVERSITY PRESS
Baton Rouge

This book was designed by Dwight Agner and composed
in Optima, a typeface designed by Hermann Zapf.

LIBRARY OF CONGRESS CATALOGING IN PUBLICATION DATA

Fanning, Michael, 1942–
  France and Sherwood Anderson: Paris notebook, 1921.
  Includes bibliographical references and index.
  CONTENTS: Anderson's summer in France.—Paris notebook, 1921 (p. 23).—
France and A story-teller's story.
  1. Anderson, Sherwood, 1876–1941—Journeys—France. 2. Anderson, Sherwood,
1876–1941. A story teller's story. I. Anderson, Sherwood, 1876–1941. Paris note-
book, 1921. 1976. II. Title.
PS3501.N4Z62   813'.5'2 [B]   74–27189
ISBN 0–8071–0176–1

This book is dedicated to people who love Sherwood Anderson because he tried so hard to tell the truth.

Contents

Preface

$\mathcal{A}$ full history of Sherwood Anderson's
life and of his standing with the critics has yet to be written.
Current consensus has Anderson a borderline major writer
whose pioneering serendipities helped to shape the twentieth-
century short story; however, signs indicate that critics of the
future—probably the near future—may well rate his writing
more highly. Whatever the eventual conclusion, the story
of this thoroughly American writer should have one chapter
that is European, and this book is intended to provide that
chapter.

In 1921, during the more consequential of his two visits to
France, Anderson kept a journal-workbook, most of which has
survived and is now deposited at the Newberry Library in
Chicago and cataloged as "Paris Notebook, 1921." Although
fragmentary, enough of the manuscript remains to reveal not
only a great deal about his experiences in France and their
influence on his thinking, but also much about the fictional
themes that were then uppermost in his mind and that were
soon to appear in such published works as *Many Marriages*,
Dark Laughter, and especially *A Story Teller's Story*. In addition, this little black notebook contains streaks of fine writing.
For all these reasons, then, I have attacked Anderson's longhand and now present the results, Paris Notebook, 1921.

I have added an introductory Chapter 1 and a critical Chapter 3. I considered Chapter 1 necessary in order to describe
the circumstances in which the notebook was written. Paris
Notebook, 1921 makes much more sense if one knows the

places Anderson went and the people he went with and met. Chapter 3 is an attempt to show the importance of the notebook and how it can be used critically. Of the three works influenced by the Paris notebook, Anderson's autobiography, *A Story Teller's Story*, is the one that has received less attention than it deserves (*Many Marriages* has received as much as it deserves, *Dark Laughter* more), so I chose to place parts of the notebook and the autobiography side by side in order to discover whether such a procedure can clarify Anderson's primary point—and in spite of the apparent rambling, there is a point—in *A Story Teller's Story*.

The generosity of a number of people contributed to this project. To begin with, there was the patience of the staffs of the Bibliothèque Nationale in Paris and the Newberry Library in Chicago. There was also the direct, friendly aid of Lewis Galantière, Ray Lewis White, Ben Kimpel, Blair Rouse, Walter B. Rideout, and Eleanor Anderson. Mrs. Anderson encouraged me in a particularly pleasant way. The most comprehensive help, however, came from my wife, Lynda, who read proof and microfilm, who bolstered my spirits and won us bread.

FRANCE AND SHERWOOD ANDERSON

1 Anderson's Summer in France

*W*ill you go to Europe on May seventeenth? Will pay your passage both ways. Have reserved berth for you and me. Wire by Sunday."[1] On January 20, 1921, Sherwood Anderson received this telegram from Paul Rosenfeld, a New York critic who had become one of Anderson's faithful guardian angels. Anderson's answer was instant and exuberant, full of that ceaseless childlike joy with which he greeted any prospect of a new adventure:

Dear Paul—

You know how happy your news made me. Of all the men I know in America it is you I should have picked to go with to Europe. This year it has been very hard for me to live in the Middle-West. I can come back here to live but I have been deeply hungry to go into old cities, see old cultural things. You have opened the door for me.

Your wire of course does not say where you want to go in Europe. I suppose of course you'll want to go to Paris.

With my passage paid I'll be able to manage—the exchange rates are favorable. I will not need to live expensively there. Surely in Paris for example Copeau can show me how to live at not too great cost. Perhaps you also know the trick of it.

· ·

O Paul I can't tell you what this chance and the opportunity it offers for companionship with you means to me. (January 23, 1921)

The Copeau mentioned in the letter was Jacques Copeau, Anderson's first French friend, the great director of the Theatre du Vieux-Colombier. According to *Sherwood Anderson's Memoirs*, Copeau and his troupe, at the bidding of Premier Clemenceau, had spent 1917–1919 in New York "for the purpose of French propaganda," [2] and just before returning home, Copeau decided out of the blue to write Sherwood Anderson in Chicago: "I had got a letter from Copeau. He had read some of my books. He was very kind. He said that some of my stories gave him a new feeling for American life. He proposed that he come to see me."

And come he did, probably arriving on May 19, 1919. Anderson, still squeezing a living from the Critchfield advertising agency, lived in a Division Street apartment, ground floor, two rooms, stark, and into this North Side flat walked the French celebrity, ready to share as a brother artist: "There was a week of close and, for me, very exciting companionship. I for the time gave up my job. Although I had already written and published several books I could not yet make my living by writing.

"It did not matter. If I have been feeling that life was unjust to me the feeling passed. I had been selected by this man as friend. He was a distinguished one. As you went about with him people stopped to look."

"Distinguished" in Anderson's account, like a Homeric epithet, attaches itself persistently to Copeau. The scantily educated Ohio boy who consciously nurtured his down-home drawl and his workingman casualness seemed to venerate automatically the eminent, the cultured. Although periodically reacting against them, he never lost his hunger for the attention of distinguished men.

One can well imagine that Chicagoans stopped to peer at the pair: Anderson with bright throat-kerchief and baggy tweeds, shaggy hair, and forty-three-year-old boy's face, ambling along beside the tall Frenchman with the bald head, gently preternatural eyes, and grand equine nose, who clamped his newly acquired corncob pipe (acquired because it was "very American") between tight lips and who sported nobly his brand-new New York clothes: gaudy tie, striped trousers, and a magnificent chartreuse overcoat. They toured and talked, enjoying especially the trolley conductors who fruitlessly tried to prevent Copeau, suddenly incapable of English, from smoking his corncob on the streetcars.

As it turned out, clothes unmade the man. In his *Memoirs*, Anderson tells us that Copeau had sunk all his spending money in a vast and garish wardrobe about which he was unabashedly vain. One night, after a session of folk singing with Carl Sandburg, Anderson and Copeau entered their flat, arm-on-shoulder, to discover that a thief, who had entered through a back window opening onto an alleyway, had made off with every stitch. The situation was "desperate"; Copeau wailed, "Oh, Sherwoodio, Sherwoodio . . . I was rich and now, you see, again I am poor . . . Oh, Sherwoodio, Sherwoodio," and wished he had hair to tear. Anderson, through the police and an underworld contact, staged frantic attempts to recover the goods but to no avail. Copeau returned apparel-impoverished to France.

It is not easy to picture the associate of Gide and Claudel so shaken about clothes, and one senses in Anderson's account in *Memoirs* the presence of Windy McPherson's son, but even at the time, in a letter written to Waldo Frank, Anderson alluded to the event in somewhat the same tone: "Jacques will tell you about his visit out here. I think he was very much distressed at what happened but that in the end he will get a dif-

ferent flavor out of it. During his visit, we became very solid
friends and I think that will last beyond anything else. It was
also delightful to see the deep friendship growing up between
him and Tennessee" (May 27, 1919).

Two years later, in a letter responding to Anderson's an-
nouncement of the Paris trip, the distinguished director himself
slipped in a wistful reference to the episode: "Hurrah! my
dear Sherwood. We are to give you the heartiest welcome. I
hope your wife will be with you. Don't fail to come now. And
let me know exactly what day, on what train, that I may be at
the station, wearing my American green hat when you set foot
on our foreign ground. I hope you will recognize me, even if
I don't wear my Chicago yellow-green overcoat" (March 23,
1921).

Anderson's second wife, Tennessee Mitchell, did go with
him on the trip, although the marriage had already, during
1920, begun to crumble. Walter Rideout, basing his picture
on interviews with a number of people who knew her, gives
this summary of Tennessee:

The independent girl from Jackson, Michigan had developed into
an attractive, sophisticated individual. "Tall, sparse, and positive,"
she was a "spirited" person with "lots of style." Her hair was medium brown with a reddish tint, and she wore unusual hats with a
special flair; indeed, all her clothes were striking and stylish. With
her willowy, if flat-chested, figure and her deliberate, flowing,
rhythmic movements, she "knew just how to wear that smock that
didn't look well on another girl." Not quite but almost beautiful,
she was elegant, poised, graceful. Even-tempered, self-sufficient,
somewhat withdrawn in manner, she was not at all cold in personality. She was quietly jolly, calmly but fully interested in whatever
was going on about her, and wittily amusing about others as well
as herself. [3]

At seventeen Tennessee had migrated to Chicago, set on leading the liberated life. There she supported herself tuning pianos

and teaching music (she later took up sculpturing), and there, in a gathering of the intelligentsia, she encountered Sherwood Anderson, who married her in 1916 in New York where the two, awaiting his divorce, had been attending a "rhythmic dance" camp in the Adirondacks.

Anderson's other companion on the trip was his benefactor, Paul Rosenfeld. Known primarily as a music and literary critic, he has been described best by fellow critic Edmund Wilson: "With his fair reddish hair and mustache, his pink cheeks and his limpid brown eyes, his good clothes which always followed the Brooks-cut college model, his presence, short though he was, had a certain authority and distinction. It was something that made Anderson call him the well-dressed man of American prose. He had a knack of turning pretty little speeches." [4]

Wilson felt that Rosenfeld was set apart from the crowd by his habit of being "genuinely considerate" and that "his affectionate and generous nature had to spend itself mainly in the sympathy that he brought to the troubles of his friends and in the tireless encouragement of talent. His judgment here was usually shrewd, his insight profound; he was tactful and unobtrusive in helping people who needed help, and he did not want thanks in return. His taking the Andersons to Europe is an example that happens to be known of the kind of thing he liked to do." Anderson was lucky to have a man of such sensibilities on and at his side.

As the summer of 1921 approached, Anderson busied about, settling travel preliminaries. On March 10 he informed Rosenfeld: "I will be sending you along the passport with my income tax receipt and all the other signatures, pictures, scrolls, etc. needed to get out of the country, by registered mail, today or tomorrow. . . . The prospect of this summer with the three of us together stirs me deeply every time I think of it.

Tennessee is a much stronger person physically than she has been since I have known her and will be a great companion." By mid-April practical preparations reached their last stages. His writing continued, but the prospect of the trip dominated: "I have no definite plans for work this year, but I am taking with me the novel, "Ohio Pagans," and a play that I am at work on. I am also hoping to do some short stories that are in the back of my mind, but I am not telling myself definitely that I will do anything except to look about and enjoy you and Tennessee" (April 12, 1921).

With passport "visaed," "return steamer ticket" paid for, and Tennessee in charge of their "one large trunk grip," Anderson felt thoroughly furnished for the jaunt, concluding the letter confidently: "I have got everything I need, I think, except a steamer rug, and I don't intend to buy one. I will borrow one from some thoughtful soul in New York before we sail. Tennessee has one."

In May, Anderson finally reached New York where, after "a round of the theatres and art gallerys" with Rosenfeld, the men joined Tennessee, and the trio boarded the French liner *Rochambeau* on the fourteenth. [5] This was to be a happy foray.

A letter written to Waldo Frank about May 20, while on board, provides a good sketch of the sea voyage and of the mood that Anderson carried to his confrontation with Europe:

The first two days of our trip were blessed with warm sunshine but now for several days it has been grey and a wet mist has blown in from the sea so that everything one wears is damp. It is a blessing to be able to get on occasion a drink of whiskey.

The people on our boat are mostly poor American artists and professional people mixed with returning French servants and small businessmen. I'm afraid the American artists are poor in more ways than one.

The constant dampness has made everyone gloomy, silent and

irritable but I am well and working every evening in the smoking room.

How shall I tell you what it means to me that America can be temporarily put away into the far distance with all this vast grey sea between it and me? I'm not bored with the slow wallowing forward of the ship (saving coal, I'm told). There is Europe toward which we go steadily. It expands, growing huge in my imagination.

And nothing dampened his imaginative expectations or his determination to open himself lovingly to the "old cultural" world, not even catarrh. Witness this bulletin, sent back to friends soon after the Le Havre landing and the arrival in Paris: "The trip over on the Rochambeau was very quiet with no one sick but in the English Channel we ran into a heavy cold fog and I got a hell of a cold in the head. We came right up to Paris and have been on the go ever since. I find myself loving Paris wholeheartedly and without reservation" (June 6, 1921).

Although no one recorded an exact itinerary of Anderson's summer in Paris, his letters and his *Memoirs*, as well as recollections of friends who were there, contain isolated facts that can be arranged into something like sequence. For instance, we know that upon Anderson's arrival Lewis Galantière, his friend from Chicago, who was working in Paris for the International Chamber of Commerce, deposited the three at the Hotel Jacob (which Ernest Hemingway, who patronized it later, characterized as clean and cheap [December, 1921]), in a solidly artistic locale on the Left Bank, near such ponderables as the Académie des Beaux-Arts, Café des Deux Magots, the Jardin du Luxembourg, and, most important, the Tuileries-Louvre complex. Galantière throughout the trip exhibited a practical flair and quietly slipped into the role of chief tour director.

Anderson wrote to friends: "We have a big double room for

about .75 American a day, and food at the smaller restaurants does not cost much. . . . After we got up to town Tennessee was smitten with a cold and laid up for a few days but is OK now again. We are but about 5 minutes walk from the Louvre and I go there almost every day" (July 6, 1921).

Rosenfeld later recounted their first walk through the Tuileries into what Anderson called "the open space fronting the Louvre": "Sherwood was overwrought on our first day in Paris. Crossing the court of the Tuileries with him I fancied he'd gotten a cinder in the eye, so vehemently was he rubbing the organ. He turned aside, leaned an arm on the pedestal of a statue. It was tears. 'I have never thought anything on earth could be so beautiful,' he stammered." [6]

Harry Hansen later quoted Anderson as saying that at that moment he was thinking specifically of the Louvre, "of the beauty of that old building and of all the tradition behind it." [7] This experience initiated a series of impressions that culminated, toward the end of his stay, in a veneration of the cathedral at Chartres; there they solidified into a revised respect for traditional art. This was to be the most influential souvenir carried home from France.

But it would be a mistake to suggest that beaux-arts or bow-tie "culture" monopolized Anderson's perception of France. Just as much as palaces and paintings, Anderson enjoyed the simple flow of French life. We find what we seek, and according to Galantière, Anderson both expected and found in Paris a variegated panorama:

Sherwood must have had his vague notion of Paris long before he saw it, just as other men have, but the first time he mentioned it to me, it was a book that brought it to his mind. "Say," he said, "Paris must be a marvelous place. I imagine it full of great wide avenues, and palaces, and beautiful women, and then, right alongside the palaces and the avenues, streets filled with dark tenements, strangled women, men with knives, poor dirty children, thousands of simple people wondering what it's all about—and not realizing at all that they're living in a place most of us would give our eye-teeth to get to."

I admitted that that was what it was like. What could I say? It is like that. [8]

The book that evoked this vision? Eugene Sue's *The Mysteries of Paris*. He had picked it up for ten cents in a Chicago secondhand bookstore and had read it mornings while headed downtown on the streetcar. Galantière continues: "Not long afterwards, Sherwood came to Paris. . . . Sherwood's attitude to the city was the same as his attitude to the book. Both swarmed with life, and it was true about the palaces standing alongside the tenements. Both were filled with light and darkness. Both—and I think this astonished Sherwood about the city—were the domain of the little man, and not of something silken and elegant and snobbish."

Anderson obviously relished casual peripatetic explorations of that "domain," either accompanied (usually by Tennessee, Rosenfeld, and Copeau) or, more frequently, alone. A French interviewer once quoted Anderson as saying, "I love life in all its forms. I think that one must always be *ready for her, open*," [9] and this attitude juts from every account of his Paris mood. He was forty-three, but he allowed a youthful blend of confidence and humility to direct the entire show. And it was a hit. Anderson bore himself about in one of his favorite images—"a bowl to be filled"—never doubting that the clear French sky concealed mounds of tart manna, prepared especially for him, awaiting only his emergence to tumble down and fill the bright hollow of each new morning. In his own words at the time: "Almost every day I go off somewhere on an adventure. I put a few francs in my pocket and just plunge into the city to find what I can" (July 6, 1921).

Frequently he found cafés, and he loved them. Later letters

of Galantière allude to two Ile Saint-Louis "bistros where we used to eat," particularly the Rendez-vous des Mariniers (November 4, 1921). And Edmund Wilson, in Paris that summer, later recalled seeing Tennessee, Rosenfeld, and Anderson in an Italian restaurant, "very clean and rather austere . . . quiet and filled with a clear twilight." [10]

But the gardens and the streets also drew him. Delicious little serendipities constantly threw themselves in his path. For example, Anderson always appreciated the Frenchman's frank, public sexuality, and in a July letter he narrated a quick, cheerily wistful brush with a bit of that frankness: "Now it is 9:30 in the morning and I am sitting under the trees in the Luxembourg Gardens. The sun is shining. A rather handsome French woman has come to sit on the other end of the bench and is flirting with me, but with my meager French the case is hopeless" (July 6, 1921).

As for the streets, just witness the good spirits and good humor of this *Memoirs* reminiscence:

> Once, in the city of Paris, I followed a man and a woman for two hours as they strolled. There was a beautiful old man with a beautiful young woman.
> They were aristocrats of life. They were both successful.
> Was it the man's daughter?
> Was he an old roué with his mistress?
> It did not matter to me. For an hour I followed them through streets, through the Luxembourg, drinking of their beauty. (433)

In addition to such adventurous meanderings, Anderson also frequently made and received housecalls. He met many; the following names occur in the sources: Léon Bazalgette, Charles le Verrier, André Gide (probable), Ezra Pound, James Joyce, Sylvia Beach, Gertrude Stein and Alice Toklas, Adrienne Monnier, Gaston Gallimard, and Marguerite Gay.

Léon Bazalgette was editor of the review *Europe*, director

of international publications for Rieder and Company and a
translator of English and American literature, most notably of
Walt Whitman. In *No Swank* Anderson tells of the day he was
first visited in his hotel room by Bazalgette, "this man with the
gray, pallid skin and the kind eyes," a "literatus" who "knew
of my scribbling"; "He had read some of my tales of my Ohio
country. 'A blessing on you for making me feel your own land
and people,' he said. 'I am glad you do not try to write like a
European.'" [11] Anderson sat for several hours talking to this
new acquaintance who, he says, epitomized the "European
man of culture. I had never before met such a one." Anderson
subsequently called on Bazalgette at his headquarters, 59 rue
Rennequin, on the Left Bank, and also met him for literary talks
in various cafés. "He told me of the French writers I did not
know and could not know because I had no French and they
had no English, what they were like, what sort of men they
were." Bazalgette later became a major publisher and even a
minor translator of Anderson, and at Bazalgette's death Anderson was to offer a eulogistic essay to his memory.

On June 11 Anderson wrote to Ben Huebsch, his publisher,
about another French literary personality:

> Things look very favorable in France for the publication of some of
> my stories and perhaps Poor White in one of the big reviews. Charles
> Le Verrier—president of a big college here—is interested and is
> working to put it through. He is an enthusiast. . . . Will you get and
> send Charles Le Verrier, 2 rue Berneville, Paris. Marching Men, Mid-
> American Chants, Winesburg Ohio.
> He may be able to help us not only here but elsewhere in Europe—
> as he is a strong man.

Apparently no publication resulted from these "strong man"
hopes. Le Verrier did, however, review several Anderson
works during the next few years.

Of Gide and Pound, Anderson left only these minuscule

synopses inserted in a letter from Paris: "Pound seems to be an empty man without fire. Of the French writers Gide is the most powerful in himself and in his influence and he is a classicist" (July 7, 1921). Since Anderson was in this letter listing people he had met, it is fairly safe to suppose that he had also met these two, although he does not directly say so. Several years later Anderson told an interviewer that he had corresponded with Gide. [12] If this is so, the correspondence has been lost.

In the same letter he added: "I saw Joyce several times, a misty gloomy Irishman." Joyce, like Bazalgette, had searched Anderson out in his rue Jacob Hotel. Their meeting went off pleasantly, full of congeniality and understanding, with Joyce, Struggling Artist, apparently quite respectful of Anderson, Established Writer. When they met again in 1927, however, all rapport had disappeared.

Anderson also made friends with Joyce's colleague, first underwriter of *Ulysses*, Sylvia Beach. Several writers have paid homage to this woman, this Good Samaritan American with her beneficent "library and bookstore" for expatriates, but Ernest Hemingway, who met her in December, has done it best. Here he reconstructs Shakespeare and Company, 12 rue de l'Odéon and pictures Miss Beach herself:

On a cold windswept street, this was a warm, cheerful place with a big stove in winter, tables and shelves of books, new books in the window, and photographs on the wall of famous writers both dead and living. The photographs all looked like snapshots and even the dead writers looked as though they had really been alive. . . .Sylvia had a lively, sharply sculptured face, brown eyes that were as alive as a small animal's and as gay as a young girl's, and wavy brown hair that was brushed back from her fine forehead and cut thick below her ears and at the line of the collar of the brown velvet jacket she wore. She had pretty legs and she was kind, cheerful and interested, and loved to make jokes and gossip. No one that I ever knew was nicer to me. [13]

Miss Beach was equally cordial to Anderson. In her memoirs, *Shakespeare and Company*, she recalls Anderson's arrival at her shop:

One day I noticed an interesting-looking man lingering on the doorstep, his eye caught by a book in the window. The book was *Winesburg, Ohio*, which had recently been published in the United States. Presently he came in and introduced himself as the author. He said he hadn't seen another copy of his book in Paris. I was not surprised, as I had looked everywhere for it myself—in one place they had said, "Anderson, Anderson? Oh, sorry, we have only the Fairy Tales." [14]

Miss Beach soon formed an amazingly sharp and sympathetic opinion of the tourist: "Anderson was a man of great charm, and I became very fond of him. I saw him as a mixture of poet and evangelist (without the preaching), with perhaps a touch of the actor. Anyhow, he was a most interesting man." What three nouns could possibly better denominate Anderson? This lady knew the man.

Sylvia remembers that Anderson's conversation in Paris often centered upon the core event of his legend: "Sherwood Anderson was full of something that had happened to him, a step he had taken, a decision he had made that was of the greatest importance in his life. I listened with suspense to the story of how he had suddenly abandoned his home and a prosperous paint business, had simply walked away one morning, shaking off forever the fetters of respectability and the burden of security."

Nine years after the fact, and the Great Rejection still looms as his soul's big moment. Throughout his life he was to relate the story over and over in various versions, reenact it in re-

jections of various wives and cities, until finally—Homer to his
own Odysseus—he was indeed to carve the mythic niche
that Elyria, Ohio, presently occupies in the history of American
literature. Every man has fidgeted behind his desk, mulling
a walkout, and Anderson apparently knew instinctively that he
had hit upon a genuine archetypal gesture; it was perhaps
largely this very knowledge that never really allowed him to
escape his escape.

Miss Beach rendered her most important service to Anderson when she escorted him to 27 rue de Fleurus and into the
household of Gertrude Stein and Alice Toklas. Here is Miss
Beach's version of the introduction:

> Sherwood told me that Gertrude Stein's writing had influenced
> him. He admired her immensely, and asked me if I would introduce
> him to her. I knew he needed no introduction, but I gladly consented
> to conduct him to the rue de Fleurus.
>
> This meeting was something of an event. Sherwood's deference
> and the admiration he expressed for her writing pleased Gertrude
> immensely. She was visibly touched. Sherwood's wife, Tennessee,
> who had accompanied us, didn't fare so well. She tried in vain to
> take part in the interesting conversation between the two writers, but
> Alice held her off.

Unknown to Tennessee, the causes of her not faring well were
Gertrude's "rules and regulations" concerning "wives." As
Miss Beach explains,

> Alice had strict orders to keep them out of the way while Gertrude
> conversed with the husbands. Tennessee was less tractable than
> most. She seated herself on a table ready to take part in the conversa-
> tion, and resisted when Alice offered to show her something on the
> other side of the sitting room. But Tennessee never succeeded in
> hearing a word of what they were saying. I pitied the thwarted lady—
> I couldn't see the necessity for the cruelty to wives that was practiced
> in the rue de Fleurus. Still, I couldn't help being amused at Alice's
> wife-proof technique.

This is one of the few anecdotes incorporating Tennessee into the cast. For some undivulged reason (apparently husband and wife were on good terms in Paris, perhaps the best in their married life, even though the marriage did in fact break up not long after the return to America), most accounts, including Anderson's, maintain heavy silence about Tennessee in Paris. Even historically the lady has been "thwarted."

Gertrude Stein placed her version of this day in *The Autobiography of Alice B. Toklas*. All her circumstantial jots and tittles do not coincide with Miss Beach's, but Miss Stein does convey the same ego-soothed gratitude, the same purring rapport observed so accurately by Miss Beach. Anderson had made a conquest, perhaps more of one than he knew. Miss Stein has her Alice-mask say:

> For some reason or other I was not present on this occasion, some domestic complication in all probability, at any rate when I did come home Gertrude Stein was moved and pleased as she has very rarely been. Gertrude Stein was in those days a little bitter, all her unpublished manuscripts, and no hope of publication or serious recognition. Sherwood Anderson came and quite simply and directly as is his way told her what he thought of her work and what it had meant to him in his development. He told it to her then and what was even rarer he told it in print immediately after. Gertrude Stein and Sherwood Anderson have always been the best of friends, but I do not believe even he realizes how much his visit meant to her.[15]

Sylvia Beach also guided Anderson into other circles. One day she introduced him to her French counterpart, Adrienne Monnier, a passionately dedicated literary caryatid who supported many writing hopefuls with all the resources of her bookstore-salon, La Maison des Amis de Livres, only a few doors down from Shakespeare and Company on the rue de l'Odéon. Besides serving scores of lightweight authors, La Maison provided a converging and counseling place for such

heavyweights as Valéry Larbaud, André Gide, and Paul
Valéry.

Adrienne Monnier was stoutish, her coloring fair, almost like a
Scandinavian's, her cheeks pink, her hair straight and brushed back
from her fine forehead. Most striking were her eyes. They were blue-
gray and slightly bulging, and reminded me of William Blake's. She
looked extremely alive. Her dress, of a style that suited her perfectly,
somebody once described as a cross between a nun's and a peasant's: a long, full skirt down to her feet, and a sort of tight-fitting
velvet waistcoat over a white silk blouse. [16]

That is Miss Beach's sketch of Miss Monnier, and here is her
short, vivid narration of the Monnier-Anderson rapproche-
ment:

I knew Adrienne would like Sherwood Anderson and that he
would like her, so I took him to her bookshop, and she was indeed
struck by him. He was immediately invited to supper. Adrienne
cooked a chicken, her specialty, and both chicken and cook made a
big hit. Anderson and Adrienne got on very well together, she speaking pidgin American, he pidgin French. They discovered that there
was a great similarity of ideas between them. In spite of the language
barrier, Adrienne understood Sherwood better than I did. Describing
him to me afterward, she said he resembled an old woman, an Indian
squaw, smoking her pipe at the fireside. Adrienne had seen squaws
at Buffalo Bill's show in Paris.

Squaw? After reading this I scrutinized the Steichen portrait
propped on my desk, pondering what I knew of Anderson from
his writing, and lo, she was right. That sag-skinned face, in
spite of its wise Tom Sawyer eyes, does project a bit of old
woman, and even at times in the writing one senses—mixed
in with a clear-headed and almost painfully profound maturity—a personality capable of being both charmingly callow
and charmingly senile.

Back in 1920 Jacques Copeau had in Paris looked after his
friend's interests by locating a prospective publisher, Gaston

Gallimard, owner of the *Nouvelle Revue Française*, and a
prospective translator, Marguerite Gay, a French lady born in
Algeria; Copeau put all three in touch, and soon Gallimard
had commissioned Mme. Gay to do *Winesburg*. This auspi-
cious beginning, however, proved deceptive; Gallimard almost immediately began procrastinating, offering various
reasons for delaying publication, and the translation was to
hang in Gallimard's limbo for seven years. Before arriving in
Paris, Anderson had written Gallimard numerous admoni-
tions, insistent and at times semithreatening, so upon arriving
he charged to a confrontation. Sylvia Beach provides these
details:

> When Anderson first came to Paris, he asked me, since he didn't
> speak French, to go with him to the Nouvelle Revue Francaise, his
> French publishers. He wanted to find out what had become of his
> works. After a rather long wait to be admitted to the editor's office,
> Sherwood got angry and threatened to break up the whole place. It
> looked for a moment as if we were going to have a regular Western.
> Then, fortunately, doors opened, and we were invited inside.

What happened in the inner sanctum we do not know, but
on July 5 a letter from Anderson to Ben Huebsch announced:
"The French translation of *Winesburg* is unsatisfactory and
will have to be done over so its appearance in French will be
delayed." This seems a strange decision in light of all the ap-
probation directed toward Mme. Gay's translation at the time.
For instance, while in Paris, Anderson wrote to Mme. Gay,
who had gone temporarily out of town: "Everyone speaks
well of the translation. Mr. Copeau and others have said they
are very good indeed" (summer, 1921). Perhaps M. Gallimard
changed everyone's mind.

As for Mme. Gay, she was to become Anderson's major
translator and to remain on impeccably genial terms with
him throughout his life. Before coming to Paris Anderson had

written Galantière, asking him to meet Mme. Gay; Galantière did so, and sent back an interesting report:

Madame Gay is a small, homely person with short legs, a big nose, a lisping, fluent and earnest speech, who is, I should say, in her thirties. But if knowledge of literature and critical feeling for it count; if you want of your translator whole-souled appreciation, accurate, instinctive insight into your meaning and honest, deep enthusiasm for your work, you have these in Madame Gay. I was greatly impressed with her intelligent conception of your stories, with her scrupulous desire to turn out only a first-rate rendering and with her courageous appreciation of the difficulties she has to surmount. She is no hack; she doesn't need to be paid for the job; she has written a few critical articles for the *Mercure de France* which were very well done; and however successfully or otherwise her translation may turn out, it will be a conscientious and honest piece of work. . . . I don't know how she got into communication with Gallimard, but she seems to have picked up the book quite by chance in the American Library here, read it, bought a copy, and been so completely bowled over by its freshness, its freedom from affectation and (as she says) ''literariness'' and its sincerity that, fearing some hack might one day translate it rottenly, she determined herself to forestall such an eventuality by doing a translation as well as she possibly could. These are almost her words, and you see the thing is being done *con amore* rather than for gain of any material kind. (February 3, 1921)

In Paris, Galantière took Anderson to meet Mme. Gay at her 20 avenue Rapp home, and Galantière's account is a gem. Galantière had always harbored misgivings about Anderson's calling himself an ''artist'' so consciously and so publicly; however, Mme. Gay's response to the person of Anderson helped Galantière eliminate some of his reservations:

When Sherwood came to Paris the first time, in 1921, she asked him to tea. He and I walked into the room together; and as she looked at him her face went white. As soon as she was free to do it, she came over to me and whispered excitedly, ''I knew he would look exactly like that! I knew it! I swear to you that, often, while working on the book or thinking about it, I have seen that man, just as he is, in my mind's eye." She was shaking all over, and as upset by her clairvoyance as if she were putting on a show for a cuckoo millionairess in Los Angeles, or for Frederick William III of Prussia, the libertine lover of table-tipping.

Now what I conclude from this true tale is that you don't have visions of favorite authors as people of ordinary looks and natures. The man Mme. Gay "saw" must be describable as an "artist"; and since Sherwood was the spit and image of the man she "saw" . . . Q.E.D. [17]

In addition to sight-seeing and visiting within Paris, Anderson and his party also conducted side trips outside the city limits. For example, he took a train, one Sunday, to the nearby village of Ville-d'Avray to meet with Mme. Gay and a critic friend of hers, M. de Maratray. Anderson also ventured north to Amiens, southwest to Chartres, southeast to Fontainebleau and Provins, and eventually northwest to Normandy on the way to London.

Artistically, the most momentous of these trips outside Paris was the pilgrimage to Chartres. Anderson spent several days there, understandably dedicating most of his time to the cathedral, and the emotions inspired by that monument to beauty imprinted themselves ineffaceably into this man who yearned so ardently to consecrate and justify himself through art. Ever since the tears before the Louvre, he had been thinking about tradition and beauty, and here these thoughts coalesced into what Rex Burbank calls "the climactic, epiphanous moment . . . when with Rosenfeld he sat entranced before the great Cathedral and found at last the symbol of imaginative fulfillment in love and art." [18]

That does not overstate the case. In 1924 Anderson was to choose this episode as the climax of his autobiography, *A Story Teller's Story*. Clearly Anderson prized his intuitions here, and immediately he began to incorporate their message of sacred craftsmanship into his private aims as an American writer.

Lewis Galantière, again, has left a captivating account of another kind of excursion: a weekend idyll to Provins. "We took a train one day, Sherwood and Tennessee and Paul, and two French friends whom I had introduced. As we were pulling out of the Gare de l'Est Sherwood stared at the enginemen and wipers and switchmen in the wide and dirty yard. 'You wouldn't think these little Frenchmen could do things like running railroads would you?' he said. He was very pleased with his remark, and chuckled." [19] The "two French friends" were probably "a French poet and his girl" that Anderson mentioned in a letter (July 6, 1921). In Provins, "a solid market town, filled on Saturdays with the farm population of the surrounding country," they toured, listening to Galantière regale them with Michelin-like history and local color, wandering about the fourteenth-century "new" town—the area closest to their hotel, the Boule d'Or—and about the "old" town, dating from the Roman occupation. The most charming incident—one that well illustrates Anderson's characteristic thought and manner in France and also one source of his satisfaction with the French—took place in a local café:

Off the square in the "old" town was a cafe, and behind the cafe a small trellised arbor. We had drinks there, and we talked, and Sherwood read some verse he'd written down in a notebook that he carried in his pocket. I don't remember the verse but I remember the voice—grave and sweet and marked by that particular accent he had ("neither" was *nother* and "either" was pronounced like *other*). I don't mean that it was a solemn session. We were sitting at a table, and we were smoking and drinking vermouth, or some such drink; and we were chatting and laughing and pointing out to one another the beauty of the prospect and the peace of the place. But in and out, the poems wove through our talk, the voice of Sherwood glided through it, and I saw suddenly that an old woman, her back really bowed down as if in a movie, stood at one end of the arbor, listening to words she could not understand. I spoke to her, and she said, "*Je ne sais pas ce qu'il dit, ce monsieur, mais il me plait.*" I told Sherwood that she said she liked him, even though she couldn't understand him, and he looked at her and laughed his friendly laugh.

"Couldn't we get a bite to eat here?" he suggested suddenly. It was about six in the evening. They said no, they never served food, had none except to feed themselves. I said something about an omelette being easy to make, a tin of sardines easy to open; but they were stubborn until Sherwood smiled at the old woman. "*Oh, oui,*" he said. "*Une omelette, qu'est-ce que c'est, une omelette?*" And he added, "Why, c'est nothing at all!" He got the omelette, got the sardines, got, I remember, some cold ham. And all this we found ready for us on the table in the arbor after a tour of the fruit and vegetable garden in which, walking beside Sherwood and not quite daring to take his arm, the old lady had shown him every plot and shown him, too, the espaliers of pears that grew along the garden wall.

The "notebook" mentioned by Galantière has survived, and Chapter 2, herein, is a complete transcription of it. It is both a journal and a writing book. The "writings" are of various kinds: tales (or "plots"), memories, a prose poem or "Testament," part of a play. This is probably typical of the way Anderson worked, keeping several projects going at a time, but the mixture may also represent the way France was evoking all kinds of creative material from him. At any rate, in his Paris Notebook, 1921 Anderson makes many observations about his French experience that coincide exactly with what we can gather from all the other sources. He considered his campaign into Gaul both an esthetic and, on another level, a *personal* success. He enjoyed the summer of 1921. In spite of some reservations, he was grateful to the French for being what they were. He wrote in July: "As for the French people—they have been fine and have done everything possible to give us a good time" (July 7, 1921). Lewis Galantière, alert as always, discerned exactly why most of the Frenchmen they met accepted Anderson so willingly:

Sherwood was happy in France, and the reason was somewhat that the French liked him so much. He was like Voltaire's Huron to them—not a Ph.D. who spoke their language correctly (which they would naively take for granted), and knew the difference between Maurice Scève and Louise Labé (which would not interest them). He carried with him, wherever he went, the authentic American culture, and he made America appear to be what at its best it is—a band of shrewd, friendly, unenvious, good-looking people; not particularly concerned to understand other men, but ready to appreciate them and very far from assuming that there wasn't room in the world for their kind and his too.

In July, Anderson wrote friends from Cabourg: "We are here in a little Norman town, about 2 hours from Havre spending a few days swimming in the sea and sleeping before going to London." After crossing the channel and spending some "hot, murky" days in London and Oxford—it was mid-August—the trio was at sea heading home.

2   Paris Notebook, 1921

*P*aris, May 28

One of the mistakes being made by the French is that they seem to take it for granted that all the rest of us, who come so gladly to France and Paris come to see and admire them.

To all the rest of us, Americans, English, South Americans, Germans, our own country and people are more attractive, more understandable. What attracts us to this place is old France. The streets here are haunted by memories. To stand for an hour in the great open space facing the building of the Louvre is worth the trip across the Atlantic. We walk thro all these streets haunted by the ghosts of great artists of the past

EDITORIAL NOTE: This chapter is the complete text of a manuscript in the Newberry Library, Chicago. The original, a small black notebook, contains seventy-four pages of Anderson's longhand.

It is both a journal (pp. 23–52 herein) and a writing-book (pp. 52–70). In editing I have chosen to transcribe exactly. Where Anderson omitted parts of words, and these omissions threaten to interrupt the sense, I have inserted my conjectures in brackets. But I have corrected nothing, so the reader must frequently assume a *sic*.

It will become quickly clear that Anderson's sense of language was fundamentally oral, not visual: he was neither a good speller nor a good punctuator; he was just a good writer.

and the present day race of Frenchmen seem as far removed from these men as ourselves.

⤳

There is something in the air of present day France, a kind of death. Before the war one felt something growing here. Now there is a kind of bitterness. I am sure it is affecting, will deeply affect French artists. Men who before the war were searching, hungering, striving, have fallen to scolding. The men I have so far met give me no sense of something growing. For example it does not seem to me that present day France could now produce a figure as naive, honest, sweet in his outlook on life as our Sandburg.

⤳

In France the art movement fall naturally into groups. One wonders if there is strength in that. Perhaps the true reason for all these group movements is fear. The individual artist being doubtful or afraid gives himself to a group hoping to gain strength there.

⤳

In Chicago and other American cities, faces seen on the streets, women going into shops, clerks going to offices, workmen going to factories, are tired faces. America wants something it cannot find. There is everywhere a sense of something like hopelessness. The old belief in material progress is lost and nothing new has yet been found.

There is however real humbleness and a strange kind of rather fine sensitiveness. P who is with me here says Americans are like fine children, badly brought up.

One senses all this more keenly here because the French seem to American eyes too alert, too sure of themselves. What

have they found to make them so self satisfied. If Paris is beautiful present day Frenchmen did not make it so.

ᔍ

I walked with a Frenchman who went to America as a boy
and has just returned here to live. He has been in Paris now for
a year. In his family, when he was a boy in America French
was continually spoken so he fell at once into the life of the
city. He spoke with me of French writing. "It is difficult for the
French prose writer to avoid the traditions of French prose" he
said. "When he tries he becomes self concious. The fine tradition of French prose is a wall so steep and high that when he
tries to crawl over he falls and breaks his bones."

ᔍ

May 30
　　No one has ever written eloquently enough of French
whiskers. Perhaps the thing cannot be done. There is sincere
abandonment. One imagines a Frenchman going to an artist
as an American about to build a house goes to an architect.
The artist lays before him a thousand designs but he is not satisfied. A new design must be created.
　　For this there is an extra charge of 60 francs. "It does not
matter. This is an important moment in life."
　　The American is afraid he will, in clothes, in manner of
walking, in facial adornment, in the style of his hat, not quite
conform to the accepted standards. He trembles lest someone
stare at him on the street.
　　With the Frenchman it is not so. It his his passion to be an
individual sharply defined, to stand forth among men.
　　The matter is not accomplished without a struggle. After a
day in the streets of Paris nothing astonishes you. On every
side are unbelievable fantastic whiskers, hats, trousers, coats.

A delightful sense of freedom is at once achieved. Deeply buried away within yourself is some passion for display. You have in secret hungered to wear a green feather in your cap, to adorn yourself with a red sash, to wear long fierce looking mustachios.

Being a born and bred American I have long looked forward to the coming of old age. "When the time comes that my work is done I shall become an old rascal, a charlatan" I have promised myself. "My days shall be spent in swaggering about, in the telling of monstrous lies, in cheating. I have pictured myself reeling thro streets clad in red pants. My whiskers have grown long and white. I shout ribald songs, swear strange oaths.

This has been my secret dream. Now I shall have to give it up. There will be nothing original in anything I can do to make myself notorious and picturesque. Alas I am Anglo Saxon. The most humble Paris cab driver can outdo me without an effort.

ᔑ

I went to dine at a resturant in old Paris, on the island. It is a place where boatmen from the Seine come to eat and drink and is called the "Marines. These little cafes are everywhere. There is a bench along the wall and a long table. Everywhere delicious food. A good dinner with wine tips and all, at the present rate of exchange costs about 60 or 70 cents in our money.

At the Marines I sat with a young French artist in prose and his misstress. They have lived together for 6 years although he is now but 24 and she a year younger. He was in the army for 4 years and in the meantime she worked, making her own living.

Now they are very poor and he is trying to make a living writing advertisments for stores.

What a sad, hurt sensitive face he has. His misstress is much

younger but there is something finely maternal in her attitude
toward him.

He tried to speak to me of the war but the little girl kept continually striving to change the subject. It is evident the matter
has become a kind of insanity with him. One refrain kept running through all his talk "They told us after the fighting we
would have our chance, that a new life would begin."

He kept asking about places in America, wild places where
life could be lived without money. There seemed a sort of
dream of a golden land of fish, berries, cool streams, deep
quiet forests.

Into the Marines came a jugler, a man of the streets. He enter-
tained us by making little funnels of paper balancing them on
his nose and burning them. When the paper funnel was burned
he continued balancing the black delicate ash, continually
talking the jargon on the streets. When someone applauded he
said sharply, "Save your hands for the work of opening your
purses."

At the opera the usher, an old French woman was dissatisfied
with the tip given her for ushering us to our seats and began to
grumble and scold. Another old woman—very neat and prim
looking, who sat beside us answered her. A cloud of words
filled the air. When the usher had fled the second old woman
spoke to us. "Im from Baltimore and can't speak a word of
French unless I'm mad through and through. Then I can give
these old blackmailers as good as they send" she explained.

James Joyce the irishman came to see us, a long, somewhat
gloomy, handsome man with beautiful hands. Everyone liked

him at once. In conversation he is very witty and the smile that lights up his gloomy face when he has said a good thing is like a light brought suddenly into a dark room. His book Ulysses, that cannot be published in America or England is to be published in Paris by Joyce himself and Miss Beach who runs an American bookstore on the Rue here. Joyce has been at work on the book for seven years and that together with all his other writing has brought him in but a few pounds. He has a wife and children and for several years has lived far from his friends and no doubt often in great poverty in Italy and Switzerland. Among all modern writers his lot has perhaps been the hardest and it may well be that his Ulysses is the most important book that will be published in this generation.

⤳

Wherever one goes in the country here in France one has a tremendious feeling of man intimate connection and contact with the earth. It is as though every grain of dust in all France had been run through the fingers of some peasant's hands. One sees very little of farming with horse and power driven implements on the American plan. Everything is more intimate. The land is the son of the peasant and has been born out of the womb of the old peasant women who work in the fields.

⤳

The future of the stage does not lie with the French. The Germans or the English will in the end do better with that art. The French is the language of declamation and good plays must not be declaimed. Perhaps the French will only succeed in playing swaggering, romantic parts.

⤳

At noon in Paris the shops close for from 1½ to 2 hours. Luncheon is a function. Everyone goes to a restaurant and later to a cafe for coffee or liquer. Little shop girls parade the street. Clerks swagger with their sticks and become, for the moment boulevardiers. There is a charming and real break in the days work.

﹥

Before I came to Paris I spent a great deal of time in the company of painters and writers who had studied or traveled in France, Germany, Italy, Spain. In their travels they had seen the work of the great painters, the "masters." How many hours have I spent hearing the work of these men discussed.

A fear grew up in me. "Too many bad painters have praised the work of Rembrandt, Rubins, Bodicelli, Leonardo and the others" I told myself. At home in America I had seen how that a painter sprang up, was proclaimed a master and within two years had been forgotten. There is such a thing as a habit of praise, a habit of acceptance.

I went with fear and trembling into the presence of the Mona Lisa, into the presence of the works of Rembrandt and the other great ones.

What happiness. In the work of every great man, long dead, I found what seemed to me greatness. In the vast forest of bad painting in the Louvre and in the other galleries here trickery has always been defeated by time. The work of the tricksters, the pretty painting hangs neglected and forgotten. The great are great because of simplicity, directness, wholeness.

﹥

I saw an exhibition of Rembrandt and others from Holland. There were many Rembrandts. Any number of old burgemeisters, associations of doctors and other stout citizens had got themselves painted.

There were two Rembrandts of which I had never seen

prints. One a golden and brown mass of figures, horses, wild half mistical scenery, a tiger staked in the foreground, a queen sitting in a golden chair and holding a sword.

Everything was suspended movement. Here was all life and none of it—something out beyond life, mystic, wonderful, caught in paint.

This from the man of the stout burgemasters.

P. and I ran back and forth from this painting to another—

A little old man dying in a bed. Beside the bed in half gloom sat a queenly woman, past youth, in full splendor of woman-hood.

Everything centered on the old man in the bed in a sea of cushions, soft feeling cushions. Georgeous heavy curtains were caught back, ready to drop over, to enfold the scene.

The old man had already slipped away, he sank into georgious dreams. Nothing human of him was left, just the sense of the dreams. Rembrandt had painted into the picture his own, half barbaric, splendid, mystic conception of death.

᠀

I have got me a place to sit in a little bare raised place above the Twillery Gardens, facing the Place de Concordat with the Rue de Rivoli at my right hand. Here no doubt the women of Paris came to knit stocking while the guillotine whacked off heads. One get a comfortable chair for the afternoon for 20 centimes and there is a broad flat wall that makes an ideal writing desk.

᠀

This has been a day of triumpth for me. I have achieved a haircut. I wear my hair somewhat long and am vain about it. An American barber cuts it ruthlessly. He is determined you shall not be a dude or a sissy. Pleading is of no use. He insists your haircut shall be exactly like very other haircut in America.

I have little French and decided I must find a barber who spoke english. I spent hours looking in vain for such a place. Finally I plunged into a French shop.

A gentle quiet little old man led me to a low chair and dressed me in a white gown. We spent 10 minutes consulting. He cut a few hairs and we consulted again. Confidence grew in me. Peace stole in on my soul. "I am going to get the first real haircut of my life" I told myself. "It will cost me a fortune to have this artist at work on me but what care I."

The haircut cost me two frances, the equivalent of 14¢ at the present exchange. Someday a wise man will import a half dozen French barbers, start a france barber shop in Chicago and gain a fortune. He can charge almost any price. We cant all come to Paris just for a haircut.

᠊ᢣ

There is a special kind of pearly clearness about French skies. Every American I see agrees with me about it. The clouds come down to you, beacon to you, something within you seems to be always on the point of floating away, into the skies. For one thing the low skyline in Paris makes the sky a more significant part of the life of the city dweller here. The pearly skies, the soft floating clouds and the fresh flowers for sale at marvelously low prices on every street corner give a constant and lovely sense of nature in the midst of the roar of the city.

᠊ᢣ

June 2

Went to walk on the river bank. A whole life goes on down here regardless of the life above, in the streets. In a long barge there are more than a hundred women doing family washings.

Other women kneel at the rivers edge beating the clothes on the stones with woden paddles.

An industry has been set up. Men women and boys have gathered the cotton from the cottonwood trees that at this time of year carpet the streets of Paris. They are combing and cleaning it and making it into mattresses. Two dozen of them are at work in the shade of some great trees. It is a little outdoor factory with a foreman walking about looking important and smoking his pipe, boys running, the combers sitting at their machines and all busy and oblivious to the life of the river and the street above.

In the river boats and barges go up and down. On each barge lives a little family and the children play up and down on the flat decks, dogs bark, the bargemans wife is preparing dinner.

There are within sight a dozen painters, men and women with their easels and stools busily painting. In the distance up the river is Notre Dame, the bridges are black with people and vehicles, here there is something quiet, pastoral. What a contrast to the dark black shores of the rivers that flow thro our American cities.

⤳

The most lovely thing happened. My hotel is in a narrow street in the midst of the old city of Paris. Last night I awoke as a clock somewhere in the neighborhood was striking three. The whole city was silent. Suddenly from far off a nightingale began singing madly. It flew into our street and for a long time sat perched on some building near at hand. The clear lovely notes rang thro the narrow street. I heard window shutters opening. Others in the street were awake—listening. The lovely bird had united all of us. For ten minutes all in the street listened carried out of our self by the sweet song of the bird.

Then it flew away, its song growing fainter and fainter as it
floated away over the roofs of the city.

〜

Dined with P on the sidewalk facing the river on the Quai
d'Orsay. Working men went past along the sidewalk. He made
two comments that have remained in my mind. First he spoke
of the French talant for work. Except the niggers on rivers in
Alabama, who sing as they work and who do an astonishing
amount of hard labor without apparent effort, I have never
seen any other people who take work for granted, as a part of
the business of life as do the French. Here in Paris and in spite
of the terrific suffering of the war one never sees the tired dis-
couraged faces so caracteristic of American cities.

P also spoke of a sense of ownership of France in the French.
It is true. It is like an immense stock company with big and
little owners. Everyone is settled down here. Men stay in the
place to which fate has assigned them. A certain freedom of
action and of living is achieved. We at home have all been fed
upon the notion that it is our individual duty to rise in the
world. No doubt this philosophy has worked out with a certain
splendor for a few individuals but on the other hand it may
have much to do with our national weariness.

Take the case of writing in America. Why should the writer
accept the standard of living of the business man. He does not
deal in monies. Why should he expect to live by the standard
set up by the dealers in monies and goods. On 1200 a year an
American writer may live. To live and have leisure and freedom to work should be for him sufficient.

One gets, as P's remark suggests a sense of other standards
here. It is perhaps because every Frenchman feels himself as
in some way having a share in France. The country goes on. In

the past beautiful things have been done. Even though a man is a waiter in a cafe under the shadow of the cathedral of Notre Dame he feels himself in some obscure way a part of the cathedral. Frenchmen built it. He is himself a Frenchman. He is a stockholder in the great company, that is France.

⤵

Everyone told me that because of the war, because of America's refusal to join in the peace, because of the action of some of the American soldiers here, for a hundred reasons I was to find the Frenchman resentful, ugly toward Americans.

It is not true. I have gone alone and with little French into all parts of Paris and into the country. Every where I have met with nothing but courtesy.

⤵

The philosophy of America, that every citizen may hope to rise to the highest estate has had a dreadful effect upon those who do not rise. There is a kind of deep resentment. The waiter in a restaurant where you try to buy as much food as possible for your money looks upon you with contempt. Here it is not so. Your desire to economize is understood by the men here who have made economizing a science. The waiter not being ashamed of his place in life is not contemptious of you because you are not rich.

⤵

In Paris there are as many bookstores as there were saloons in Chicago before prohibition. Imagine the 1st ward in Chicago with every saloon of the old days turned into a bookstore. The latin quarter here is like that.

⤵

Went to walk with K B [1] who I knew years ago in America. He has no money but is living in a beautiful apartment overlooking the old fortification and the Cluny hills. Some friend has given him the apartment for the summer. Such things are always happening to him, always will be happening to him. He is the most delightful man I have ever known because he has no center of his own, no strong individual passion possesses him. For an hour, an evening, a day, a month he gives himself completely to the man or woman he is with.

I spoke of the American negro and my hope that some day an American artist would see the beauty of their caracters and persons and write or paint that beauty so that the negro should also see it. K. B became at once inflamed with the idea—was all sympathy and understanding. Tomorrow he will have forgotten the negro of America forever.

The man has lived in almost every country in Europe and has become thoroughly European. He spoke with enthusiasm of the Russian caracter. "Paris and all western Europe is but the front door of America," he said. "Out there something new is growing up."

When we had talked for some time another man came in who at once began to condemn the Russian revolution and all social revolutions. "When revolutions come art and the impulse toward beauty dies. All men think of improving their material welfare."

It was an interesting moment. K B wavered. In some way the revolutionary idea had taken hold of him. Then his passion for swinging off his own center and giving himself to the impulses of others took hold on him and his loyalty to the Russians and their social experiment became weak.

I have known K B for years. All men and most women who come into contact with him love him. It be perhaps that they love what of themselves they see reflected in him.

Walked with P in the garden of the Palais Royal. We talked of America, both agreeing that while American cities were all comparatively ugly nothing could tempt us to come away to live permanently in a European city. We agreed that it was in some way a man's part to play the hand fate had delt him in life.

I wondered if—were a man born over here—his note in life would be essentially different. P thought not. "There is something men are striving for now that is bigger than nationalities" he said. "The effort to go down into the hidden parts of ourselves and find out about people down there hasn't much to do with nationalities."

ᕀ

I saw some of Rodan's statues. All I have seen of them makes me feel he is a man a little too literary, intellectual. There is something a little forced. Perhaps he did not wholly give himself to his work.

ᕀ

In American the fight a man makes to realize himself, the fight all men have made there is against nature. Here there is a sense of humanity that is like nature. Nature is subject to man but when men have lived in one place thousands of years there is in the very air a sense of humanity become as impersonal as our prairies.

ᕀ

In a cafe a Parisian said to me, "It is as bad not to marry as to marry. Both plans in life are unsuccessful."

ᕀ

Many French poets produce little poetry. They are forever

sitting in cafes and develope marvelously the gift of conversation. Into the practice of that gift they pour themselves.

⤳

June 4

In the early morning went to walk in the narrow streets back of the Academy. Here are many little shops showing the work of younger painters for sale. A war had broken out between two unknown and obscure schools of painting. Four young men from one of the schools had come to attack certain advocates of an oposing school. The battle was fought out on one of the narrow streets. There young men had fortified themselves in a room on the second floor occupied by one of their members. They had as weapons to hurl at their opponents in the street eggs, oranges, pieces of furniture and dishes. The party in the street were supplied with similar munitients. The war raged furiously. Wild cries arose. One of the party in the street got hit fair on the breast with an egg. People from all the neighboring houses and from shops ran into the street and joined in the outcry. The battle lasted until practically all the furniture and dishes had been thrown out of the room above and the broken fragments had been fired back. Two windows were broken.

The battle ended in a handsome way. Two women came along the narrow street pushing a push cart. As there was nothing more to be thrown the man with the egg on his bosom ran into the street and threw up his hands. "Peace in the name of French womanhood" he shouted and the bystanders cheered.

⤳

Went to sit in a cafe where I got into talk with a fat man of 35. He is a German from Milwaukee Wis. At 20 he set out for

Europe having been provided with money by his fellow citizens who were very good to him. It was his dream to blow the cornet as it had never been blown before, to make of it a classical instrument. With what hopes he set out. It cost him $60 to go from New York to Hamburg. He did not care. He was full of disgust with the so called kings of the cornet who went about America playing in halls.

When he was in Germany he for a time forgot the cornet. At night he could not sleep. Such thoughts he had.

He began to arrange his thoughts into chapters. It was a book, a book of philosophy.

Everything cost money. He wrote the book in English and German. Everything was set down. Then he lived at low cost and got money with which to have it typewritten. He had the books, both German and English copies bound in leather. There were more than 400 pages. A girl help him with the puntiation and the spelling of words.

It is a book of philosophy, economics. No editor will publish it. They say no I don't care to do so but he is not unhappy. Life is not unpleasant for him.

He went to France and when he had acquired the French language he put the book into France.

He has a brother in South Chicago who plays in an orchestra. Also he has a sister in Milwaukee who has sent him her picture taken in a bathing suit.

If things were not as they are he would go to America.

There is one thing he would like—to go to America and give concerts showing what can be done with the cornet as a classical instrument. If he could do it there is no doubt he would have great success.

There is no doubt the French people are different from others. The thing shows itself in the woman. He has taken him a French wife who makes designs for wall paper and cloth and the covers of books. Everything she makes is quickly sold. He himself plays the cornet in a moving picture palace. His life is not a dissatisfied one.

If his wife were not French perhaps she would take the money they have saved and send him on a concert tour to America to show what can be done with the cornet as a classical instrument. Being French she will not do it.

"Oh well," she says "Money does not grow on bushes there. You do not pick it up in the streets.

No doubt he will have to give up some of his dreams. Perhaps he will find a rich American who will take him on such a tour. It would result in something grand. He would play 25 pieces all written by those who have won the Prix de Rome. Nothing like it has ever been seen.

It would be nice also if such a man would have published his book on philosophy and economics. It would show him as he is, a well rounded man.

He would like to receive me at his home but I must come there between the hours of 1 and 3, otherwise he may be away sitting in a cafe. His wife is younger than he and pretty. The difficulty is she knows no English words and my few French words would not suffice with her.

⤳

On the streets of Paris are thousands of men, women and boys competing with horses. They are harnessed to heavily loaded carts and sometimes struggle horrible as they dragg the carts up hill over rough cobblestone streets.

⤳

Everywhere in France the spirit of Napoleon is alive. One feels so the man and his power on every street. In the bookstore windows everywhere ar prints, Napoleon making a victorious pease, Napoleon winning battles, signing papers, flourishing swords, riding fiery horses.

On the boat going to France I saw an American who once had a great name. In the smoking room I sat near him and listened to his conversation.

A devilish thought came. "Suppose after all Napoleon like that—made by advertising" I thought. I said something of the sort to a Frenchman. It was not a fortunate remark.

‿

June 6

Lunch under trees in an old country town. A young French poet, very sensitive, not well. He was wounded three time in the war and also gassed. A broad-mouthed peasant girl waited on us, brought us wine and flowers. Everything the poet has written sinse the war began he now intends to destroy unprinted. "It was" he declares, "a time when no sweetness came up out of French soil, when the blossoms of trees had no fragrance. He could speak of it but little. There is a dark celler filled with dead things within him.

He was in a sector where there were many Americans. He found them childlike, "children who could kill" he said.

Later he was in a hospital beside a wounded man, also an American. His comrads thought him insane but to the French poet he was filled with charm. The man, he declared was striving to save himself from the insanity of acceptance of ugliness.

"Well he talked wildly. There was something sweet and fine. The American childishness had strength and beauty in it. The wounded man took a pocketknife out of his pocket. He talked. What a thing was a pocketknife. It could cut apples as one sat on the tongue of a wagon in a farm in Iowa. It could cut the bands with which wheat was bound into bundles. It could cut a roap by which a boat was tied to a wharf so that one could float away down a river, past towns, past farms, past forests.

The wounded American talked for hours of the possibilities of sweet things brought into existence by the stroke of the blade of a pocketknife. He talked of a piece of cloth, of a fragment of wood picked up on the floor. All the others thought him insane. The French poet thought his babbling had saved them both from the real insanity.

On a bridge over the Seine—a young working man with his sweetheart, a tall strong young daughter of France. They stood with arms about each other looking up the river. Occasionally they kissed oblivious to the thousands of people passing, seemingly equally oblivious of them. Very pretty. One sees lovers everywhere going straight on being lovers without self conciousness.

At the restaurant out of doors in the country. Several men in our party were attracted to the broad mouthed daughter of the house who served us. When we came away I rather self-conciously waiting until I thought no one looking then turned to blow her a kiss. She stood under a tree near to the entrance to the garden. When I turned around I found two or three other men doing what I had been doing and like myself hoping they were unobserved.

On an old house at Provence—this inscription.

Jean Fouquet
An honest and Faithfull Magistrate.
Decapitated 1353

June 10

The splendid horses of Paris pulling the great wheeled carts. Great hogsheads of wine, grain piled high in brown sacks. The wheels of some of the carts are as high as the door of a church. Often the great horses are hitched tandem—three, four—six, ten. The horses are not castrated. There is fire and life in them. The drivers walk in the streets swinging their long whips which they crack like rifle shots.

O, the great horses. O the shrewd lunging sharp tongued drivers.

These are my people. There is the sharp acid smell of sweat. These men love the great breasted stallions as do I. They are not afraid. They do not castrate. Here is life more noble than anything machinery has yet achieved.

⤴

Other European nations may die but the French will be a long time dying. There are some who would lead them to militarism, to be again conquorors.

The thing in France that will be a long time dying has nothing to do with war and conquest. Perhaps the nation will be greatest when all hope of conquest is finally lost.

⤴

If I lived in France I would choose to be a teamster, flourishing a long whip and driving six stallions hitched to a great cart piled high with wine barrels.

⤴

To stand on the Pont Arcole at night, when there is a new moon. In Paris in summer the darkness comes late falling softly. Along the wharfs boys are playing. Three tall boys are teaching a youngster to fight with his fists. They run laughing up and throwing down their arm dodge his blows. Their heads rock back and forth skillfully. Three girls from a house on the rue d'Arcole have come to stand beside me. They are young working girls in cheap dresses and join in the fun going on below. The boys are not unconcious of their presence. The little fellow strikes out more furiously. In the uncertain light the heads of the older boys, dodging the blows are like the heads of serpents. Suddenly a blow goes home with a sharp thud to the face. The little fellow dances with joy. The girls cry out with joy.

To the left but a short block away Notre Dame. The great bulk of it seems to lift itself up into the sky. It is a great floating body of lace woven of stone.

In front, to the left also the spire of Sainte Chapelle. In this soft glowing light the crown of thorns motif is accentuated. It is a growing thing, reaching up and up. It is almost dark now but in the fleecy clouds to the west the red still shows. Blood of Christ. The crown of thorns pressed down. The blood spurting. The spire is so lovely now, in this light the throat hurts.

Here is life all about. Little prostitutes decked out in cheap feathers hurry away out of streets behind you on the right bank. Men with their wives, fat wives come to lean on the railings and on the stone coping above the river. There is a drunken man whose wife is scolding. He laughs loudly.

Two prostitutes come close. There is a man with them, a striking young dandy. He is the pimp of the short fat prostitute. She is trying to tease him, playing clumsily. Perhaps the breath taking beauty of the place and the hour has awakened something. She pinces his arm and it hurt and whirling suddenly he kicks her on the buttocks, soundly.

She squeals with the pain of it but continues the play. Putting her two hands on the cheeks of her buttocks, she runs along the bridge squealing.

The other woman—she is tall and slender and wears her hat down over one ear and has no lover and is concious of me. She also puts her hands to her nether cheeks and squeals, looking back over her shoulder and laughing.

↬

A night of love and love making. You go into the little park back of Notre Dame, you stand on many bridges, you go to see how that, when the moonlight falls on it, the Louvre looks a white frozen things. Everywhere lovers. Lips are being pressed to lips. Womens bodies are being pressed closely against the bodies of men. The lovers are in all the little dark places, on the bridges, on the stairway leading down to the dark river. A young girls body is held tightly against the trunk of a tree in the shadows of Notre Dame. A bearded man is holding it there. He presses his great body against it. The lovers are all silent.

↬

When the workmen were building the great church to Our Lady of Paris nights came. Old fervors died and new fervors were born. The new fervor ran down into the fingers of workmen. It expressed itself in the gargoyles grinning down now at the lovers under the trees.

↬

Notre Dame is too huge. The fervor could not run on. Only in Sainte Chapelle is the impulse quite pure and alone.

↬

Two American college proffessor on the Q' d'Orsay. One is tall the other short. The short one has bad eyes and knocks against people and things. He presses close against his tall

friend. They are talking of the effect of the coming of
phiscoanalasys on art in America.

ↄ

American cities have no Louvres, no Saint Chapelles, no
Notre Dames, no Cluny but we have there a constant inflow of
new people and impulses. Perhaps it would take a long time
for a really new impulse to penetrate France.

ↄ

Although America is inhabited by every race under the sun so
that when one meets a fellow American he must always ask,
"Of what blood are your people, we are peculiarly intolerant.
Paris is the true cosmopolitan city. Here all races may meet
and loose the sense of race. Just now the Germans are not
looked on with favor but the Chinese, the negro, the Japan-
nees, all these go about freely. One often sees negro dining in
restaurants and walking in the streets with their white sweet-
hearts. The sight attracts no attention. In an American city it
would cause a riot. Perhaps being sure of its race lines the
French can afford to be generous and careless.

ↄ

One is constantly struck with the nearness of Parisian life to
the country. Wagon loads of hay go thro the streets, peasants
from the country are driving in in carts, the vegetables and
fruits are peculiarly fresh and delicious. The morning dew is
still on these berries now for sale from a little wheeled cart
under my window.

ↄ

I am charmed with the cries of the street vendors. Each has
got a refrain, a skirl of music into his cry. It is sweet to lie in bed

in the morning and hear the bird like voices crying regarding the shapening of knives, shining of shoes, selling of vegetables.

꙳

Americans make a great mistake in being timid and in staying about hotels where other Americans live. Here, as everywhere it is the common peope who receive you most generously, who are delighted to help you in your difficulties with the language, who take you into their everyday life.

A Frenchman and his wife who have lived in America have been entertaining some weathy American friends. The American men wanted to see the night life of Paris and have spent huge sums doing it. What they have got is a specially prepared stage set for them. They and their wives who have been in the big shops throwing money about have been cheated gloriously. My friend the Frenchman and his wife are rather pleased at what has happened to these Americans and I sympathise with their feeling.

꙳

A French girl leaning out a window I saw in a village, two women working in a field, their bodies bending and unbending slowly, the librare at the chateau at Fontainbleau, to sit in the far corner of the court late in the afternoon when everyone has gone away and look at Saint Chapelle, the spire of Saint Chapelle, seen at night from a bridge, Jacques in the early morning with women sewing in the little park and carts rattling past in the street, an old workman washing his shirt in the Seine, his bare back very strong, a beautifully dressed aristocrat among women who alighted from a motor, the Louve at night, in the late afternoon, in the morning, the rose window on the side of Notre Dame that faces the river—this seen at

night with the three ghostly stone figures stepping down from
above, an old woman with a pipe in her mouth at the tiller of a
barge on the Seine, the upper chapel of S. C. in the early afternoon with the light flooding in, a garden on the hill in the old
village of Provence, the lovely wood carving on doors in many
old buildings, the singing of a nightingale at night in the city.
To sit in a cafe drinking and reading, now and then to glance
up at people passing. To accept France as you accept America,
thinking of it only as a place you dont understand—to drink
beer with men and women you love, in a cafe, under a giant
tree, in the forest of Fountainbleau.

⤴

There are places that must be seen alone. The exclamations of
people terrify, they are like whiplashes on tender flesh. Even
intelligent comment is hurtful. One does not recieve the
caress of beauty thro the intellect. It creeps upon you or flashes
down on you like a stroke of lightning. There is the necessity of
readjustment, of rebuilding something within. Every new and
beautiful thing seen destroys while it seals [heals?]. You are a
tender hurt, shattered thing emerging from the womb of some
great mother. Silence and solitude the sweet, the golden thing.
Long after perhaps we shall speak to each other.

⤴

In a castle where kings, emperors, queens, the mistresses of
kings have lived. The guide escorts a troop of people into a
room where one of these women has lived. He makes little oily
jokes. The women in the party giggle. The men think thoughts
of lying in beds with queens. There is a combined effort to
invade the lives of these queen, mistresses of queen, kings,
emperors. It is as though we all threw mud at them. There is a

deep fear in all of us. We are afraid that they great may after all
have been great.

꙳

When I visit the places about which Mark Twain wrote in his
innocence Abroad and realize how he often made a labor-
ously wrought joke of men's effort toward beauty in order to
please and flatter American readers it is difficult for me to to
retain the love aroused in me by his writing of Huckelberry
Finn.

꙳

When beauty comes off it seems to justify always the terrible
cost. What would it mean if every American child could see
Saint Chapelle, Chartres cathedral, the library in the palace at
Fountainbleau. Those thousands of peasants coming up from
the field, a kings desire being gratified, a hope of heaven where
all men lead equally beautiful lives, stone laid on stone, beg-
gars whining, stone on stone, thousands laboring terrible,
stone being carved, the animal side of men coming out, the
gargoyles carved, grinning things looking down on misery and
on the strutting of kings, the mistresses of kings coming in
carriages to look, driving in the morning with sleep heavy eyes
after nights in heavy curtained beds, the men working silently
perhaps, doggedly, thousands of men, crops being neglected,
no sanitation, disease running among them. Stone on stone,
years passing, now and then beautiful moments, stone carved
beautifully with abandon, terror, and beauty, something to
stand up for ages. Stone on stone. There is beauty achieved.
Who shall say it is not all sacred, terrible, wonderful.

꙳

June—still
   Cloudy. My life and yours in America. Doing what we think

we must do. Old things too, we know little about. A desire in us to caress old things, then perhaps to sneer at them. They cost too much we think.

↝

In a cafe again. There are two young negroes, with books in their hands talking with two white men students in the Boulevard Saint Germain, near the district of the great schools. Near me, at another table a white American woman—fat.

Her daughter, pale, with staring eyes. There is deep anger. "I saw a nigger with a white girl and the white girl's mother, walking openly in the street. My fingers itched to have hold of a gun and shoot—all them." The head of the fat mother nodding up and down. She agrees without thought, from habit.

↝

A man, an artist, an American who has lived in Paris for 20 years. To dine with him. Three times during the evening he said the same thing. "A man is of no importance who hasn't his roots deep in his native soil" There was something tragic in his insistence. "Can't you go back?" I asked. "Not now. I have blown about too long. I'm an empty thing."

There was in his face something shrewd, yankee but his accent was English. All evening I kept remembering certain, dry, shrewd horse owners I knew long ago. He was like a man who has taken horses from track to track, all over the world, but has never won a race.

↝

French writers are badly paid and from all I hear France is very provincial in its attitude toward outside men and outside ideas. The French writer, of the better sort (the artist) expects no profit from writing. Many are clerks or have government jobs. There is in the American attitude something much more generous, fine. Here the arts are honored but the better artists starve. In America there is little knowledge of what good art is but there is an eager generosity toward the artist.

⤳

In the older churches one sees constantly sculpture and painting that is closely alied to modern art. The Sorbonne show—everyone agrees is dead. It is only the moderns and the old old men of the middle ages who seem to approach life and beauty.

⤳

To the house of an old French family where we sat all afternoon speaking of worms in the vineyards of the south, of hot sun on the hills, of olive trees in the plains and of the clear French light that has had so much to do with making France the home of painting.

⤳

In the night when all is silent a cart passes through the narrow streets of the old city and the hoofs of the horses ring out and echo and reechoe along the walls like cannon shots.

⤳

The Quatre Arts Ball has been held. It is a sex orgy that would be impossible in an Anglo Saxon civilization but nevertheless I am quite sure that many of the partisipants, perhaps a majority of the men present were English or Americans.

⤳

June 13
　　To an upper class French home—the home of a French banker.—An Englishman with his French wife was present.

I got down on the floor and tried to explain the game of base-
ball, the fame of Ty Cob, Babe Ruth and others. They were all
polite and tried to speak English. Little cakes were served and
the young Englishman played the violin. It was just such an
evening as one might have spent in the home of a well to do
banker in Iowa.

꙳

It apparently is not true, as I have often heard, that the French
disliked the American soldiers. During the war and afterward
the people all became sick of the sight of uniformed men. It
was really war sickness. From all I have heard the common
American soldier left a deep impressing of something rather
fine. "They were the only soldiers that came who loved to play
with our children" the French said. One hears that story everywhere. "The Americans loved our children."

꙳

"The days were wonderful and
the nights were wonderful
and the life was pleasant." [2]

"The spoon was set six. Eight was a biginning It began. Ear-
rings are good to breed. Breed that." [3]

Imagain a strong woman with legs like stone pillars sitting in
a room hung thick with Picassos. Formerly there were many
Matisse and ———— too but except 2 ———— these have gone.

The woman is the very symbol of health and streng. She
laughs. She smokes cigaretts. She tell stories with an American
shrewdness in getting the tang and the kick into the telling.

Gertrude Stein is perhaps 45 and for 10 or perhaps 15 years
she has been sitting at a desk in the room writing such sen-
tences as those above. When her first book Three Lives was
published (at her own expense and later when Tender Buttons

appeared a little flame of interest and amusement flared up in America. Newspaper paragraphers quoted her. It became for a time the thing, in smart literary circles to give readings from her works.

To dine is west. —[4]

A great revolution in the art of words had begun and was being passed over with a laugh.

Gertrude Stein has always been laughed at. Years ago when her work first fell under my eyes and I was startled and profoundly stirred by its significants I made inquiry concerning her. Strange stories came out of Paris. She was a fat woman, very languid lying on a couch, people came into the room and she stared at them with strange cold eyes. There was a strange power in her by the exercise of which she was able to[5]

ᓯ

A Woman's Evening

Mary-at work in an office—early Oct—Sat noon. Elinor Rysdale comes in. They lunch—

Go to call ostensible on a woman musician. Her husband a painter meets them in disabile. They go in. Conversation between Elinor and painter in which Mary takes no party. E really in love with painter but denying it to herself. He talks ruthlessly—upsetting her. M & E go out into the street in silence. What E things. What M thinks.

M goes to her apartment. A young man Edward Springer comes, G. B. type.[6] His wife in Paris. He wanted to be an artist. Couldn't. A crüper [croupier?]. He talks giving details of his married life. Declares love. Now or never. His splendid moment. The curd [cur?] into the street.

Mary—to take the half thing? Maud Bonan comes—again the half thing. The ride into the country in a ford. Blankets in

the car. The stop by the roadside. Maud's approach. M rejection. The ride home. 2 am. M in bed.

❧

The Story of a Day.

Or Two Acquaintances.
Or the Land of Romance.

On a railroad journey, going to Kansas to write a book telling of the life of a man who manufactures incubators. The book is to make something of a hero of the man. He is a poor farm boy who saved his pennies. He became interested in the incubation of eggs, nailed boxes together, studied the matter of moisture. Once for 10 days he went without sleep. Everyone thought him insane. In his experiments he burned his father's farm. Became an engineer at a grist mill.

At last his dreams became facts. He began to man[ufacture] in[cubators]. How wonderful. They were sup[erior] to all other incubators. He built a small fac[tory]. It became larger. The town grew.

Now it has been arrainged that the town council pay for a book of his life & I am engaged to write it. The idea has been sug[gested] by a Chicago ad[vertising] man. I am engaged because I have my name up as a writer. It is so writers live and prosper in Amer.

On the train, going to the town I sit alone in the smoker. A hot dry day in Aug.

At a little town a man comes in and we fall into talk. He is a man of fifty, boyish body, iron grey hair, a mustache.

He begins talking of himself and when we reach the town I invite him to dine with me. He objects because of the cost to me. We have sand[wiches] and coffee at a r[ail]r[oad] place.

The eve is young and he has evidently no desire to go home. We walk out along the r r tracks where the sun is going down over the great plains.

The story of his youth. The son of a banker who owns cattle rances in the west. Father is being cheated by the foreman of the ranch. The son goes to straighten things out. The foreman. The cowboys. His con[cern] for them. The for[eman] has a dau[ghter]—and the young mans pas[sions] have been aroused. The fore sees how thins are going. He is not unwilling [that] something hap[pen]. The young man and woman are left alone in the ranch house at night. He goes to the girls room. She lies still. He becomes her lover.

What the r[ancher] had not counted on was that she loved him. She tells him just how his father is being cheated. Cattle are being driven south & sold into Texas. There is a place to go. There is a little town on the Mex border. Tomorrow a 1000 cattle are to be secretly driven away by one Hank, a dark and dangerous man.

The young man is of true American stuff. On the next morning he leaves the ranch. The For questions his daughter. No he has not come to her but in the morn he has told her he is [needed at?] home and is going home.

It is enough. The foreman laughs ha ha.

The boy rides all day and at night takes a train. He arrives in D. Wires his father. 10000 sent by tel. He charters a cattle train, flies to the little town on the Mex border. Goes into a little resturant. There sits H drinking. He does not notice the boy who strowls past him. Steals his gun. Holds him up with his own gun. The cattle are outside the town. They are driven in and put in the cars. Hank and his asso[ciates] are taken before the sheriff. H makes con[fession]—involving the foreman.

The boy goes tri[umphantly] to his father. He is a hero. A

beautiful so[ciety] woman wants to marry him but at the last moment, just on the day before the wed he is walking alone in the city park when he thinks of the fore daug in the ranch house.

That eve he gets a letter from her. Her f[ather] is in jail. She is home[less]. Is working as a waitress in a little hotel. She is with child.

He goes to his father. Marry beneath your sta[tion] and I disinherit you.

Defying all he goes to the girl. His father dies leaving all his money to a younger son. He might have fought the will but was too proud to fight.

The walk homeward with the man met in the train. The voices inside the house.

On the next day.

The man—a small ner[vous] man, with dead grey eyes. He goes listlessly about. The adv man from C has come and takes me about. He tells me the story of the in[cubator] man and I go to the hotel to write. In the eve I go to the I[ncubator] man's house to dine. The wife and daughter. The talk of books. At 8 o'clock I declare I am full of the desire to write the life. Do not dis[turb] me I say to the ad man.

The man of the train comes again. We again walk out of the town. Once when he was a young man, befor he came west his father sent him to travel in Europe. One night he was in a little hill villiage in Italy. Some men came in and there was drink. The young man offered to drink with all in the room. A con[versation] began. The daughter of the inn[keeper] brought the drinks. She was beau[tiful], with dark hair and eyes that burned with a strange fire.

The men all sat by a long tabl, the inn keeper among them. His wife was dead. When the drinking had been going on for a time the daughter seized an op[portunity] to whisper to the young man. Your life is in danger. These men are all ban[dits], murderer.

Fear made him trem[ble] inwardly but out[wardly] he was calm. He had to be. There was no bravery. All was necessary. The drinking went on and on and the dark bearded men sat glar[ing] at the young man. A strange thing hap[pened]. He drank and drank but was unaffected. The men began to admire him. They got constantly more and more drunk. Songs cries. The young man sat pale determined, drink & drink. The wine was dark brown—very strong & bitter.

At last the men began to fall senseless on the floor. He was saved. The girl escorted him out of the inn, sad[dled] his horse. As he was about to ride away feeling p[roud] and s[trong] a thought came to him. He had [not] drunk w[ine] at all. The girl had given him cold coffee, thin by water and with some[thing] in it to make it taste bitter.

He got off his horse and walked to the in door. In[side] the f[ather] and his band lay on the floor as dead. A moon came up. The girl stood under a little vine colored trellis. Her face in the moonlight. I loved you when you came in at the door. I shall never love another.

The ride in the night. The return next day. The father, his band and the girl gone. The long search alone in the mountains. Sick of a fever. The dead love that shall never die.

I am to take a mid-[night] train. The walk to the man's house. Good night. The look in at the window. The con[versation] with the son.

Sitting abord the train. The adver man. I have been walking & think of the wonder[ful] story of the makers of incubators. Into berth. The towns sliding past

⤴

I am sitting at a window, high above the street, at a busy cor-
ner in a modern city. The river of people below runs on and on.
There is a dull, heavy, insistent sound—iron striking iron.
The bell ringing of the modern age men at thier work.

One speed. Two speeds—a mad rush. Little humans on the
sidewalks, in the eddies, gathered before windows of stores.

Black faces, white faces.

I have dropped something out at the open window. I have
dropped it, still I hold it. An invisable cord connects the part of
me sitting here with the part of me that has gone down there.
I am a fisher at the river bank.

You shall be fishers of men.

You shall be fishers of women.

The women of the street hold up bowls to be filled. Some of
the bowls are sweet with the sweetness of clean flesh. Others
are foul with the foulness of flesh no longer sweet.

I am of the blood of those who have denied the sweetness of
flesh. I am out of the loins of thouse who foul flesh with
unbelief.

The invisable cord between my visable self sitting here and
the invisable me cast down there is tough and strong. I go
down and come up.

Fishers of men.

Fishers of women.

My desire is a great as a mountain. It is as swift as a thought.

I would fill the bowls at the fountain of life. If the cord breaks
between me and the life I love let me remain down there in
the street with the clean and the unclean. Let my dead body
sit here as a reproach to those who befoul life with unbelief.

Men fishers.

Women fishers.

Going and coming.

I dreamed I went far on a long road with two men. One was Christ, white and humble, walking with bowed head. His hands were slender and white. His face was slender and white. He knew all but could not bear knowing all.

I had a hand on his shoulder and the other hand about the waist of one strong and brown. Mustles playing over strong bones. Flesh smelling keen and with a sweet acid flavor. Brown hair floating. Swift legs running. Hard eyes gleaming. Laughter on lips.

We kept marching and I looking small. Looking to one— then to the other.

Fishers of women only—all of us.

We marched in the city. We went where iron struck against iron. We peered into still faces, white faces. Lips met. Clothes were torn.

i had beauty shown me in the faces of women.

When bowls were filled beauty came. My companions embraced each other. They embraced me.

We went filling bowls. Scattering ourselves. Throwing ourselves into the stream.

Arms went. White faces went. Hard firm flesh playing on bones grew hard and fell away.

We hid ourselves into the river. We sumerged ourselves into the river. We were crushed under the great bowls, the numberless bowls.

The cord held.

Fishers of men.

Fishers of women.

The cord held and we climbed back here, becoming one. We became myself sitting here dreaming of men, dreaming of the coming of men.

I sit here now. One speed—two speeds—a mad rush—

Little humans on the sidewalks, in the eddies, gathered before windows of stores.

White faces black faces.

Bowls held up to the windows.

ᔱ

A Forbidden Friendship

In what a strange place I met her and what a notable thing the meeting was to me.

One of those impossible meeting of circumstances and events happened.

First of all she was a negro girl, an American negro girl met it London. Let me try to gather up the threads of the event.

During the year before I was for some six months in Alabama. I went there to be alone and to write down certain impressins plucked out of life in the form of stories and novels. I had thought there, in the midst of black folk I should be able to seperate myself from the wruts of life as I knew it.

For a week, two weeks I worked steadily at what I conceived to be my own task not looking at the life about me. All about me life went up and down. My cabin was on a strip of beach and beyond the beach the mouth of a river came down into the bay.[7] Banking the two shores of the river were wharfs where boats came in and tied up to recive an discharge cargo and from where boats went out to the ports of the world. A few fruit steamers came and went but for the most part the ships coming and going in and out of that harbor were sailing ship come to get sawed lumber from the mills up the river.

There was something very leisurely and calm about that traffic. A boat came in and tied up. The crew lingered about or went up into the old city on the river and the bay. From inland down river by smaller boats or by train came a steady stream and the sweet smelling lumber. The boats turn came to be loaded and it was loaded, very efficiently and as I at the time tho[ught] very leisurely by the black boys.

I was a northern man and there was much about that fellow, the black man at work I didn't understand. Had I not been told about efficency. Men who sang as the swung great timbers aboard a ship were not the hustlers of my own land. For me labor was something else, a dark grim, silent thing. These singing negroes, loading ships with a song and a laugh were not laborers. They were children, black irresponsible children. Had not my men of the n told me so. Was I not now being told the same thing by white men of the south.

As for the black man—I didn't want particularly to think of him. I thought I preferred not to think of him.

And the days went and the ship were loaded and song dropped down the bay to me and I went to walk, not on the wharfs among the blacks but down along the bay to the place where their song could no longer be heard.

From the bay I turned inland at a little place where northerners, well to do men from O, I Ill had come to the far s[outh] place to make themselves homes for certain winter months. How ugly and smug the little house were and what names they had. The Dovecote. Westwood. Idlehours Moss Manor etc. The names were painted on board and stuck up over frail, cheaply flung together verandas on which tired old men sat staring with tired vacant eyes from M M into the staring windows of Westwood.

I hurried past that place and into a great forest of pine trees and the song of the blacks I had left at the wharfs loading the ships began again. I was in a great turp[entine] forest and the blacks were harvesting the pungent strong sap of the pine trees. Parties of 3 or 4 went thro the forest emp[tying] the little bleed-

ing cups into great pails and the pails into can in wagons. All
the trees had been wounded and they all bled. It was a land
of pain I had come into and there in the midst of the pain were
the sing[ing] negroes.

I sat on a log, away from them where they did not see me
and listened.

There was something in the blacks I had not understood,
could not understand. They were alone in the forest then with
no whites about. Of my own presence they knew nothing.

And they were singing and the thing not understandable to
me was in their song. It floated near me and then as the little
group of men at work went deeper and deeper into the for[est]
and away from me the song went with them. After a time only
a faint fragrance of it ran along the ground under the trees to me
sitting and wondering on my fallen log.

I went home to my cabin then. An awakening had come
to me.

I began to seek something but what I sought was very elu-
sive, is very illlusive. I do not at all think I have found it.

                    ⌐

To live that half day, hour, minute even. To throw all art purpose, solemn ends aside. To see all America in the leaf that
dances before the nose as you sit in a cafe in a villiage in France
or in a park in London.

I have loved this woman with her soft eyes, firm breast,
strong thighs. My seed has run into her. Shall it not run into
seas and skies.

I have this flood to pour forth. My riders. Mount your horses,
ride desperately in night roads. Tear all flood gates away.

I saw in the eyes of men a thing as tender, sweet, clear as
ever looked out of mothers eyes, at me.

I would be one man to give unqualified love to men, women, children.

A little twisted girl came to me at night wanting my seed to carry away in her basket.

I refused and now hells door clanks open for me too.

That was yesterday's night with which I in all honor have nothing to do now.

I am the shadow of my self as this dark spot dancing on the ground here is the shadow of some living leaf in a living tree rooted deep down in darkness, in earth, dark, damp, sour, sweet earth.

I come in vital splendor now to accompany my own shadow in life, play with it, love it, march with it to the sound of drums.

If I live now this day, hour, part of this minute only you coming long after me shall kneel and kiss some running shadow thinking it me.

What I want to say is that the running shadow you shall kiss is me and that I have love of you.

⤳

Mother Winters had got suddenly old.[8] She did not understand what had happened and perhaps did not try. She was only 36 but how long her life had been.

Three years before something had happened. First the cords of her neck grew tired and ached then the aching went down into her back and arms. All over her body were certain little veins she had never been conscious of before that were now being drawn taut. They were getting ready to snap and the process was agonizing. At night M W had dreams. She was a farm girl again and was leading a cow along a path at the edge of a deep ravine. Suddenly the cow whirled and sprang out of the path to hang by the rope above the great black empty space. She hung on furiously, all the mustles of her arms aching. The ground crumbled beneath her feet. In the great eyes of the cow there was an appeal that filled her with desperate determination. How furiously the mustles of her body ached. Now she also was about to fall down, down. She awoke.

At another time she dreamed she had gone to a fair and stood in a great building filled with animals, sheep, giant pigs, bulls with great thick necks, cows with slender legs and soft eyes. A shouting began. She was alone in the building and there was no air. The animals became restless. The great bulls pawed, throwing up clouds of dust and bellowed hoarsely. The pigs squealed as she had so often heard them squeal at the moment of death, at pig killing time on the farm.

In the dreams she was always a young girl in a torn dress and was always frightened. Her hands were soiled and hardened with labor so that she wanted to hide them behind her back.

And there she was in the center of the great building and there was no air to breath. Now all the animals squealed, bellowed and bleated loudly, pitiously. Within her own breast something hurt pitiously.

Outside the building shouts arose from a thousand throats. She tried to think, to understand. The dust kicked up by the animals, all now leaping and dancing furiously, in an agony choked her.

There was a door fastened by a heavy bold of iron. She ran to it. It must be lifted. Then the glad light and the sweet air of the out of doors would be let into the building. There was life, joy, happiness, for herself and all the im[prisoned] animals to be got by lifting the heavy iron bar.

She could not reach it. Although she stood on tiptoe and strained terrible she could just with the point of her fingers touch the bar underneath. It was cold, as winter, as ice in the washtub by the back door of the Win house in winter. The bar she could not reach was as cold as death. It was death. One raised death out of its sockets on the great door and then joy and light came in. She strained and strained, reaching up and up. Then she was exhausted and fell on the dust, on the floor. Again she awoke.

The Winters house stood back from the road three miles from town. There was a creek and a pond and beside the pond was an old sawmill, a building without sides, just a sheet iron roof held up by poles and now sagging like an old tent. Former-ly there was a millrace and a wheel and in the spring and fall power enough to saw great logs but the damn had partly fallen down and Pa Winters had bought a steam engine.

There wasn't much timber sawing to do. Now and then some money might be made cutting fire wood or fence posts, but most of the time the saw mill stood empty and silent.

Pa Winters went in there and sat on a log, smoking a pipe. He was a tall man with a red beard, very silent and filled with wrath that was bottled up inside him.

What was he angry about He himself did not know. He hadn't always been so. In his youth he was a roistering fellow, always getting drunk in town, fighting with other men at country dances. Then his father was the sullen silent one while he continually made a great noise, shouting, singing, whis-tling, swearing round oaths. There was a kind of love in it. When he was a young fellow hauling logs out of the forest P. Winters often swore at his team in a long [loud?] voice in order to hear his voice run thro the forest under the trees. He did it to his horses, his dog, and a cow he was driving along a lane.

Then his father died, he got possession of the sawmill and

he married Ma Winters. He got Ma Winters out of a German family named Swartz where she was employed. The girl herself hardly knew how she got there. Her mother had also work for the Swartz's and she never saw her father. He was a farm hand who went away to see about taking up land in the far west and never came back. When she was 10 years old she got s pox, brought it home to the swartz house from a country s[tore] and gave it to her mother who died.

And then—there she was, a servant in the Swartz house. Ma Swartz was large silent & sullen and there was no other child and the child found her comradship among animals. When Ma S went to town for sup[plies] and Pa Swartz to work in the fields, she went to the barn followed by the Swartz dog. The horses having a day of rest, two colts in a small shed, an old sow with a litter of pigs, a flock of sheep in a field that came down to the barn, all ran crying to greet her. It was not feeding time but she got oats out of a bin & fed the horses. Then she ran into the garden back of the house and pulled veg[etables] which she fed to the pigs, the colts, the sheep. The cows with their calves were away in a distant field but as she stood on the raised grown by the barn door one of them threw up its head and bawled. The sound ran over the hills to her. It was a call to her. The cows also loved her.

Ma S did not intend to be unkind but Agnes was neither a servant nor a daughter so she did the work of a ser without pay. The clothes she wore, everything was given to her. It was a hard possition. She asked for nothing. She got little.

When she was 17 years old, tall and with a thin sm[all] face some[thing] hap[pened]. On a summer day, on Sat, Ma S had driven away to town taking with her eggs and but[ter] to be exchanged for the weeks supply of groceries.

↬

Play

Making a Man

1st scene—A

Boy or young man—17—In the living room & kitchen of a small workingman's apartment on Chi. west side.

Mother—a lean tense tired looking woman of 40 is cooking something on a stove.

There is a younger son who has been ill & is slowly convalescent sitting in a rocking chair by the stove.

Conversation between mother & older son about life.

Why will he not work in a factory This going out to pool rooms—hanging about with tough boys. It will lead to no good end.

Talk of the gangs of young roughs—robbing, stealing automobiles. They land in prison, get hung.

Y. M.—I'd rather be hung than be a man of the fac[tory] like dad.

Look here Ma. Didn't you ever want anything better than you got here. Think of working all your days and never having fine clothes, jewels, fast auto.

I'll tell you what Ma. If I turn out a robber dont you be sur-[prised]. I may get in the Carney gang. I could get in now if I wanted too. Only reason I dont I guess is that they are the real thing.—sticking up little shops etc.

M C—Oh Tom. Would you bury your mothers old head in sorrow etc.

Bah Ma. Dont talk bunk. Say would you like me to become a stupid man like Pa.

I guess he wasn't always so stupid eh. Say what about when you mar[ried] him Ma. He had some[thing] to him then eh. I'll bet I know what. He tho[ught] may[be] he would rise up in the fac[tory]. Get to be fore[man] then sup[erintendent] eh. Well you and he talked of that once. What do you think now.

Well hes gone and joined the S[ocialist] party. I've lis[tened] to his guff until I'm sick of it. brotherly love stuff. bah.

I tell you what Ma, I know what hap[pened] to Pa. I worked down there in that shoe shop six months didn't I. The noon hours sit on the wall, the talk. ah.

I'll tell you what there's some[thing] better about being a thief or better yet a rob[ber].

Made to ride home from the fac. Crowded car—cattle. What men would do.

You & little Frank here might as well find out where I stand. Say Ma I stole some[thing] today but I'm pretty ashamed. It was just a litle sneak thief job—I did [not] have any money, aint had any for 9 weeks now. I saw this box of colored chalk on a counter in a store.

Takes it out. Begins to draw a huge grotes[que] design on the wall.

M cries. Won't have T life spoiled.

T con[tinues] to draw on wall—becomes absorbed.

Father comes in—long talk scolding. Wont you ever become a man.

I'm more of a man now than you are—the trouble is I wont let them make a thing of me. Quarrel fight. T. knocks his father uncon[scious]. M runs in. What have you done now. I've put an end to this life anyway—bah.

Scene—stage B.

Man comes out of a stairway & runs away. In a few min[utes] is fol[lowed] by a young w[oman], she angry. She stares after him.

Line—The dirty sneak.

Another woman comes along. What's the matter.

1st woman tells a tale. She has had a man in her room. He paid her 3 dol and she put it in her coat pocket & then hung the coat up. When he was gone she found out he had stolen the money. Scolds and scolds. Wish Jack would get him. I'd like to see him pull his gat and shoot all such sneaks full of holes.

T comes along—Here comes W-Grapes. You watch me string him.

1st wo[man] dis[appears] up stairway. Second wo waits for T. He comes along and she touches him on the arm. Why dont you never have anything to do with the Janes?

3 scene—

Business men—bootlegger.

T. much law breaking.

4—The quarrel in the gang.

5—T shoots policeman.

6—Advertising scene.

7—Prison scene, escape.

8—The upper room.

T & the six police.

⤸

Embarkation

A woman of thirty five in a great shed like building at Havre. We all stood about saying little things, expressing our little annoyances. We were going back to our places in the Un States after a summer in Europe and there had been a ruling by our gov[ernment] by which we had to take the same test, be subjected to the same humiliations as the em[igrants] who were to travel third class.

Everyone grew indignant. There were two young women, students who walked up and down scolding. We have to be vac[cinated] too? they said. It's outrageous. An old man with a grey beard, a coll prof as I afterward learned got an American ex[press?] agent into a corner and whis[pered] to him. "I'm going to try to fix it" he whis when he came over to where I stood. I'll give someone 50 f. You'll see. I'll get out of this. The ex[press? agent] was doubtful. He went away shaking his head.

There was a long roped in place where the em[igrants] stood like cattle in a pen, waiting the ordeal that was to take place in the room above. I went to look at them.

On the whole they are good stuff I thought.

The mass of people moved forward a little. An idea came to me.

ᔄ

Adventures in Color

The subject came up between us as such subjects do come up. He was a steamboat pilot on an Alabama river and I sat with him in the pilot house, a glass enclosed affair in which we sailed along at about the level of the tops of trees.

He was a small yellow skinned man about fifty years of age, such a fellow as might have run a hardware store in my Ohio home town, a silent fellow very capable and as the river was out of its banks kept constantly on the alert.

There was a pardner, a one-armed talkative man who took turns at the wheel with the small man but as I did not fancy him I stayed out of the pilot house when he was on duty. As I was the only passenger on the boat going all the way up river and back I had become something of a privaledged caracter and as I had my water color box with me I sometimes sat on the deck painting, a fact that lent a touch of romance to my figure.

It was during that trip I first began to sense the American negro and the subject that came up between the pilot and myself concerned the feeling of white men toward negroe women.

"I've heard a good many stories. What about them? What's going on?," I asked.

The boat was nearing a landing and when my acquaintance began to curse, in what seemed to me an unnecessarily vile way I thought something terrible must have happened down below and jumping to my feet ran to look.

Everything seemed all right. The current was very swift but we made headway against it and the long sidewalk-like landing stage was perched in the air, ready to be dropped at just the correct spot at a word from the mate. A group of negro boys stood ready to lower away and another boy balanced himself far out on the end of the landing stage, holding a heavy rope and ready to leap ashore and make fast to a convenient tree.

3   France and *A Story-Teller's Story*

*A*ll of Sherwood Anderson's essential impressions of France were formed in 1921, and already while in Paris he was beginning to work with the materials—the satirically romantic tale, the memoirs, even the prose poem—that he would very soon draw together in the book that was published in 1924 as *A Story Teller's Story*. A comparison of Paris Notebook, 1921 and *A Story Teller's Story* provides interesting insight into how the trip influenced the book, for material from the notebook was very consciously utilized. What had been scattered observations in the notebook coalesced in the autobiography into unified definitive statements of what France had meant to Anderson.

On the title page of *A Story Teller's Story* Anderson describes his book as "The tale of an American writer's journey through his own imaginative world and through the world of facts." It is indeed a book about a man's imagination and about how it affects his unique identity as an American, as an individual touching other individuals, and most importantly, as an artist. *A Story Teller's Story* offers a particularly rich opportunity to dig into this subject, for not only is imagination its topic;

imagination is also its method, and this combination means
that the reader can, throughout, compare Anderson's practice
with his preaching.

As Anderson approaches the end of the autobiography, he
chooses to summarize his story's meaning by condensing it
all into a life-reviewing reverie that he says took place back
in 1921 as he and Paul Rosenfeld paid homage to Chartres
Cathedral, a monument that has appeared early in the book
(Bk. II) and has developed steadily into the ideal embodiment
of his imagination, "the beauty shrine of my life."[1]

I am always having those moments of checking up like a miser
closing the shutters of his house at night to count his gold before
he goes to bed and although there are many notes on which I might
close this book on my imaginative life in America, it seems to me
good enough to close it just there as I sat that day before Chartres
Cathedral beside a man I had come to love and in the presence of
that cathedral that had made me more deeply happy than any other
work of art I had ever seen. (407)

One of Anderson's daydreaming streams begins with the
realization that the cathedral's surroundings, in contrast to its
own consummate beauty, exhibit unavoidable vulgarity: "The
cathedral before me was faced on one side by ugly sheds, such
as some railroad company might have put up on the shores
of a lake facing a city of mid-America" (399). Watching the
tourists—fellow mid-Westerners—drive their automobiles
hurriedly up to and away from the cathedral, Anderson in his
thoughts flows back to that mid-America, to the physical
ugliness of its industrialism and to the moral ugliness of its
business ethnic. He recalls his own earlier participation "in
modern American life, cheating some, lying a good deal,
scheming, being hurt by others, hurting others" (398), and he
recalls that his earliest gestures toward the beautiful, toward
the comforts of craft, came as a direct reaction against the

ugliness that surrounded him: "After years of striving to get
money, to get power, to be successful, I had found in the end
well-nigh perfect contentment in looking and listening, in
sitting lost in some little corner, writing, trying to write all
down. 'A little worm in the fair apple of progress,' I had called
myself laughing—the American laugh" (399). The facts of
American life were unpleasant, so he would escape them by
creating and worshiping beautiful objects; his art, he realizes
at Chartres, originally grew from "the desire for something . . .
to glisten and shine outside the muddle of life" (408).

A Story Teller's Story was translated into French and, according to Sisley Huddleston, an expatriate in France at the
time, "was published with considerable success in Paris."[2]
The French were indeed interested in Anderson's autobiography, and astute comments were made by several Frenchmen, particularly Régis Michaud, Léon-Gabriel Gros, Charles
Cestre, Lewis Galantière, and André Berge. The most vocal of
these, Régis Michaud, expended a great deal of breath on
Anderson's reaction to American ugliness; he felt that Anderson's intense love of the old crafts had been motivated by a
nostalgic fear that America's esthetic sense would disappear
into a morass of standardization, that Anderson "wants, like
Ruskin and William Morris, to help us re-discover, 'through
all the broken surface distractions of modern life, that old
love of craft out of which culture springs.'"[3] In support of his
observation, Michaud quotes Anderson praising "the harness-
maker, the carriage-builder," etc., for their "sensual love of
materials" (*STS*, 14). "The coming of modern industrialism,"
says Anderson in this passage, has replaced this love with
"speed, houses, city apartment houses with shining bathroom
floors, the Ford, the Twentieth Century Limited, the World
War, jazz, the movies."

In *A Story Teller's Story*, Anderson always presents Chartres as a symbol of that ancient craftsmanship so alien to these modern values. In one such presentation, Chartres enters an ironic dream in which Anderson has been transported from his Chicago rooming house—alive or dead?—into a mysterious gigantic edifice: "A feeling of being very small in the presence of something vast has taken possession of me. Can it be Chartres, the Virgin, the woman, God's woman? What am I talking about? I cannot be in the cathedral at Chartres. . . . I am an American and if I am dead my spirit must now be in a large half-ruined and empty factory, a factory with cracks in the walls where the work of the builders was scamped, as nearly all building was scamped in my time" (185–86).

Sitting before the cathedral (Bk. IV), Anderson recalls his character Hugh McVey, from *Poor White*, who drew comfort from looking at "a little handful of shining stones": "To the child man, the American who was hero of my book and, I thought, to myself and to many other American men I had seen, they were something a little permanent. They were beautiful and strange at the moment and would be still beautiful and strange after a week, a month, a year" (408). A man's imagination must dwell on beauty in order to construct a stable defense against the encroachment of tawdry transience. A passage in Paris Notebook, 1921 makes much the same point. A French poet tells of an American hospitalized during the war. The American, his imagination churning, had talked incessantly of his pocketknife and of "the possibilities of sweet things brought into existence by the stroke of the blade of a pocket-knife" (PN, 41). The motivation for such wild talk was plain to the poet: "The man," he declared, "was striving to save himself from the insanity of ugliness." This, it seems to me, describes exactly the source of Anderson's own impetus toward *fancy*—a word, by the way, that is Anderson's all-encompassing synonym for imagination, creativity, art.

Most French critics interpreted Anderson's complaints about America's materialism to be the most valuable theme in the entire autobiography; as Léon-Gabriel Gros put it, "The passages that one remembers readily are those . . . in which Sherwood, with his apparent bonhomie, makes his voice heard in the general indictment of materialistic civilization." [4]

Anderson himself, in an interview given to a French magazine, emphasized the book's social negations. The interviewer reports that Anderson said, "The book *A Story Teller's Story* has had some success . . . because in it I defended an artisan against standardization. My compatriots adore being criticized." [5] There is no doubt that, during the early twenties, the writing period of this autobiography, Anderson was upset by America's failures. Paris Notebook, 1921, one source in point, shows that French culture helped him clarify, by contrast, what he regretted about his own. In these notes he compares, for example, Paris' "pastoral" beauty with America's urban ugliness (32). He recalls the "tired faces" of American urban workers and the ineffectualness of their "old belief in material progress" (24). With the resentment and weariness brought on by the American drive "to rise in the world" Anderson contrasts the ease, the continuity, the stability and the self-respect resulting from the French system, where "men stay in the place to which fate has assigned them" (33). In manners and dress Anderson contrasts the Frenchman's "passion to be an individual sharply defined" with the American's cowed need to "conform to the accepted standards" (25).

These are the same fundamental complaints that most French critics spotted as central to *A Story Teller's Story*; I think, however, that the reader who overemphasizes Anderson's anti-Americanism may well miss what is really the book's main theme: the confrontation between fancy and fact. Materialism is only one—albeit an obtrusive one—of these facts; it does not fill the entire picture, and nowhere in the autobiography does Anderson speak as a partisan in a revolutionary movement to restructure society, as Michaud and Gros imply he does. On the social level all that Anderson suggests in *A Story Teller's Story* is for the artist to detach himself from the marketplace. As he says in Paris Notebook, 1921: "Why should the writer accept the standard of living of the business man" (33).

"Escapes" dominate *A Story Teller's Story*. They begin in Book I with the embarrassing ham-and-exaggeration Civil War yarn that his father cooks up about evading southern captors. It is the same sort of preposterous yarn that Anderson had experimented with in Paris Notebook (53–56), and which he employs in the autobiography to satirize and to explain the romantic tale, Hollywood, the formula story, American failure of sensibility, his father, himself. Anderson said this about how and from what he and his father were running: "And so the Civil War became for him the canvas, the tubes of paint, the brushes with which he painted his pictures. Perhaps one might better say his own imagination was the brush and the Civil War his paint pot. And he did have a fancy for escapes, as I myself have always had. My own tales, told and untold, are full of escapes—by water in the dark and in a leaky boat, escapes from situations, escapes from dullness, from pretense" (*STS*, 59–60).

The "situation" escape that stands out above all others in *A Story Teller's Story* is, of course, Anderson's dramatic abandoning of his Elyria paint factory. He inflates this gesture, as a matter of fact, into the prime symbol of his refusal to accept those business standards; and, perhaps even more important, in the process he manages to evoke parallels to all the other major escapes contained in the autobiography—childhood's escape into make-believe fancy, the artist's escape into the fancy of craftsmanship, his later temporary escape into European culture, and his final loving escape (again through fancy) into the lives of others. Anderson, in *A Story Teller's Story*, tells the classic version of the Elyria story, and he clearly presents himself as "le type," in Galantière's word, [6] of American Man caught in Archetypal Dilemma.

Régis Michaud has a fascinating interpretation of this episode: "Let us not forget this escape. We will find it again in his books. . . . It is one phase of conversion. . . . The ceaseless renewal of existence is one of the dogmas of his gospel. Escape, sudden uprooting, are in his novels, just as in the lives of the saints, a necessary condition for moral perfection and sanctification, the access to a new life. 'Leave all and follow me,' declares the voice to which his heroes surrender themselves." [7] Michaud's insight merits underscoring. Anderson's reactions against American society led him to no genuinely social solution; they led him rather to a supremely private and quasi-religious conversion, to an inward recoil and recommitment similar to the experience of the saint and expressed in terms of the artist.

This may be one reason Anderson chooses Chartres as his artistic ideal; it combines love of beauty with love of God, two ideals America has missed: "They built the cathedral of Chartres to the glory of God and we really intended building here a land to the glory of Man, and thought we were doing it too. That was our intention and the affair only blew up in the process, or got perverted, because Man, even the brave and the free Man, is somewhat a less worthy object of glorification than God" (301). In Book IV, Anderson and Paul Rosenfeld identify themselves with the devout: "The stooped figures of old Frenchwomen with shawls about their shoulders kept hurrying across the open space, going into the cathedral to worship. My friend and I were also worshiping at the cathedral, had been doing that for days" (400). Granted, *A Story Teller's Story* involves social problems; still the attempt to fit the book into a solely social mold often causes critics to lose sight of the importance of its religious and esthetic fervor. Anderson's implied preachments may at times begin socially, but they always end with the artist-writer alone in his room facing the holy whiteness of his paper.

At Chartres, Anderson says, "Now, for a few years, I had been looking abroad. . . . I had taken a second leap from New York to Paris" (*STS*, 399). The last half of *A Story Teller's Story* is indeed carried by this move "East," to New York and to Europe, climaxing at Chartres. In Book IV, Note IX, Anderson relates some of the excitement with which he approached Europe, his motives for going, and what he expected to find there: "One goes from Chicago to New York on a modern train very quickly but in the short time while the train is tearing along, while one sleeps and awakens once, one cuts the distance between oneself and Europe immeasurably. To the American, and in spite of the later disillusionment brought by the World War, Europe remained the old home of the crafts. Even as the train goes eastward in one's own country, there is an inner ferment of excitement" (390).

Through his mind march the names of his cultural heroes: Turgenev, Gogol, Fielding, Cervantes, Defoe, Balzac. Anticipation rises: "To the man of the American West how much the East means. How deeply buried the great European craftsmen had been in the soil out of which they had come. How intimately they had known their own peoples and with what infinite delicacy and understanding they had spoken out of them. As one sat in the train one found oneself bitterly condemning many of our own older craftsmen for selling out their inheritances, for selling out the younger men, too" (390).

Around 1920 Anderson was as dissatisfied with his own

craftsmanship as he was with America's. He felt a strong need for "a basis of self-criticism" (*STS*, 395), and to find it he decided to "go looking for the masters" (385). In New York he asked himself: "Had I myself come to New York, half wanting to go on to Europe and not quite daring? . . . Something pulled. It was so difficult to understand life and the impulses of life here" (392). A major element of this drive toward Europe was plainly a nostalgia for the old, a deep conservative need to contact roots: "Being an American in a new land and facing a new time, did I want even what Europe must have meant in the hearts of many of the older men who had talked to the boy on the streets of an Ohio town? Was there something in me that, at the moment, went wandering back through the blood of my ancestors, through the blood of the ancestors of the men about me—to England, to Italy, Sweden, Russia, France, Germany—older places, older towns, older impulses?" (128, 129).

Here, then, is what Anderson brought to France—basically a hope that his own threatened devotion to beauty would be revitalized by communing with the products of centuries of such devotion.

This theme, it may be helpful to note, occupies an important position not only in *A Story Teller's Story* but in *Paris Notebook, 1921* as well. On page 49 of the latter, for instance, he speaks of "a desire in us to caress old things," and most of the scenes and topics bear out exactly that desire. In the very first entry he declares unequivocally that the value of France abides not in modern Frenchmen but in "the ghosts of great artists of the past" (23) met at the Louvre, Notre Dame, Sainte-Chapelle, Chartres.

Anderson is chiefly fascinated by what he believed to be the intense relationship that existed between the old craftsmen and their materials. For example, in speculating about the building of the cathedrals (PN, 44, 48), he conceives as "sacred, terrible, wonderful" the moment when "fervor ran down into the fingers of the workmen" and on into the stone their fingers were carving. In *A Story Teller's Story*, in the Chartres section, he ponders that same mysterious bond between a craftsman's imagination and his materials. With the curious eye of a taleteller he watches an American woman weep as she leans against the cathedral door, and as he watches, he muses: "What had been in the hearts of the workmen who once leaned over the same door carving it? They were fellows who had imaginations that flamed up. 'Always wood for carvers to carve, always little flashing things to stir the souls of painters, always the tangle of human lives for the tale-tellers to mull over, dream over,' I told myself" (401).

One is here at the center of Anderson's love of craft. The material of his craft is words, and Régis Michaud has described Anderson's own almost talismanic rapport with these words. Illustrating from *A Story Teller's Story*, Michaud follows Anderson as he walks the streets and fixes on a man or woman whose secret he wants to know. The walk ends in Anderson's room with this realization: "Well! The white page is there to reveal it to you!" [8] Sitting before the page, says Michaud, Anderson plays with words until they become like a painter's colors, until he can almost touch them. At this point Michaud breaks out with an observation bulging with potential: "It is probably this poetic and mallarmean notion of the virgin paper, the sentient sheet on which words actually live, that inspired Anderson with a special interest in the surrealistic writings of Mme. Gertrude Stein." [9]

Lewis Galantière, in commenting on the same passage of the autobiography, observes exactly the same tilt of Anderson's imagination: "We know that precisely like a surrealist, he very early fell in love with words, and that it was an imperious need to play with them that drove him to scribble away in his cheap

little flat in Chicago."[10] Apparently what Michaud and Galantière mean to emphasize by "mallarmean" and "surrealist" is
the old Parnassian principle, as transmitted through Mallarmé
and on into the surrealists, of the poet as pure artisan concentrating exclusively on the *plastic* function of words. As Michaud further explains it, Anderson "set about the business
of writing for the same reason that one does bookbinding,
engraving, or gilding: a love of handling beautiful material."[11]

As for Gertrude Stein, she was a primary agency through
which this tradition reached Anderson. As early as 1921, in
the Paris notebook, Anderson records that her "great revolution in the art of words" had "profoundly stirred" him (52).
In *A Story Teller's Story*, describing his first reaction to *Tender
Buttons*, he explains why he was profoundly stirred: "How it
had excited me! Here was something purely experimental
and dealing in words separated from sense—in the ordinary
meaning of the word sense—an approach I was sure the poets
must often be compelled to make. Was it an approach that
would help me? I decided to try it" (359). This attempt, this
conscientious playing with "new and strange combinations of
words," resulted in what he calls "a new familiarity with the
words of my own vocabulary. I became a little conscious
where before I had been unconscious. Perhaps it was then I
really fell in love with words" (362). "Reading Miss Stein,"
he says, "had made me feel words as more living things" (374).

As this influence set in, however, it did not create a genuine
partisan of art-for-art's sake. A formidable, barely bridgeable
chasm separates Mallarmé from Anderson. Nevertheless, one
did affect the other. For one thing, as he says above, Anderson for the first time became "conscious." His thinking
opened to the independent value of word sound and word
texture as almost magical components of an incantation, as
living integers that one manipulates in order to realign reality,

to charm the chaos into some kind of at least temporary sub-
mission. Put another way, for Anderson, style itself began to
exist. His early writing seems to have been composed of blunt
meanderings, instinctive lurches at self-expression informed
by only a subliminal awareness of the possibilities of his
medium; after *Tender Buttons*, style moved to the front, and
he believed himself more an artist than ever before; he became
a man solidly possessed of a craft. Anderson always seemed to
yearn to be a plastic artisan; he gave himself earnestly, for
instance, to painting. Miss Stein had now taught him the plastic
dimension of words, and like a painter or an old cathedral
carver he now saw and caressed his materials. He even began
to love the feel of paper and pencil; he was working with his
hands.

I remember that the first time I read Anderson I was gripped
not by what was being said but by how. I had never before
read prose so powerfully simple, so slow, and so sure; the style
alone asserted a potent honesty. Very probably, Anderson
would never have been able to marshal his words this effec-
tively without having first passed through Miss Stein's word-
for-word's-sake baptism. Anderson's literature is, above all,
people, but the savor of those people would never have made
it to the written page if Anderson's imagination had not at some
point acquired this intensely craftsmanlike focus.

In Paris, as he communed with the "great artists of the past,"
Anderson formed more and more distinctly his own private
conception of beauty. Every day, it seemed, something in-
choate broke into expression. For instance, when he met the
"masters" at the Louvre, as he relates in Paris Notebook,
1921, although he had feared being disappointed he was
overwhelmed by the joy of recognizing what he knew to be
great art: "What happiness. In the work of every great man,

long dead, I found what seemed to me greatness. In the vast forest of bad painting in the Louvre and in the other galleries here trickery has always been defeated by time. The work of the tricksters, the pretty painting hangs neglected and forgotten. The great are great because of simplicity, directness, wholeness" (29).

In Book I of *A Story Teller's Story*, Anderson relates an episode in which his older brother steals a neighbor's hatchet. That night, as the two boys lie in bed waiting for their mother, Anderson in his mind instinctively composes "slick plausible excuses" (20) for what his brother has done. Anderson the adult reflects: "In all my after years I shall have to struggle against a tendency toward slickness and plausibility in myself" (19). It occurs to Anderson that his father, with all his self-delusion and his sentimental tall tales, has lived with the same tendency. His mother and brother, on the other hand, have not. When the mother comes and asks about the theft, the brother answers "fairly and squarely. . . . 'I wanted the hatchet and so I took it—that's what I did.'" Mrs. Anderson responds, "It doesn't take much of a fellow to snatch a hatchet." As he listens to this conversation, the boy Anderson cries, because he senses that in these two "there was a kind of directness and simplicity that father and all fellows, who like myself are of the same breed with him, can never quite achieve" (24).

Setting this episode beside the Paris notebook description of the Louvre painting, one notices immediately that what Anderson admires in the masters is exactly the quality he admires in his mother and brother, and that this quality diametrically opposes his own natural inclinations. Anderson's esthetic credo demanded a facing of facts without resorting to extenuating flourish, to the whitewashing "slickness" of the lesser artist, to the "trickery" which seeks the easy way out of unpleasantness. This was the ideal that Anderson admired in others and pursued in his own work, and I think it is a significant revelation that in this pursuit he was forced constantly to deny himself; he was engaged in a vehement struggle not only with the values of his society but also with his own nature.

James Schevill has said that Anderson's definition of beauty in the above notebook passage "is very similar to Milton's famous credo for poetry, 'simple, sensuous, passionate.'" [12] Although at first glance comparison with such a giant may seem impertinent, it is after all valid, for in his best tales Anderson does at least approach the kind of power that transforms *Paradise Lost* from a potentially "slick" use of myth into a hard and vital collision with the facts of life, into an art object that does not shun but accepts the "dust and heat," that does indeed face its material with "simplicity, directness, wholeness." In Anderson's case this seems a definite step up from the early idea of art as escape. Beauty still combats ugliness; now, however, the beauty operates not away from but directly *through* that ugliness.

The same Louvre section of Paris Notebook, 1921 further elaborates the concept. In describing a Rembrandt painting, Anderson says, "Everything was suspended movement. Here was all life and none of it—something out beyond life, mystic, wonderful, caught in paint" (30).

Elsewhere in Anderson's writing we see this creation of "suspended movement" asserted to be the artist's fundamental function. For instance, in the Chartres section of *A Story Teller's Story*, Anderson watches an American with his two women—one apparently a wife, the other a lover—and Anderson realizes how quickly the drama unfolding before his eyes will pass; he first wishes life could stand still, then corrects himself: "As though anything ever stood still anywhere. It was the artist's business to make it stand still—well, just to fix the moment, in a painting, in a tale, in a poem'' (403).

The paradoxical second sentence of the preceding quotation from Paris Notebook, 1921 derives directly from this effort to halt mutability. Anderson speaks of ''something out beyond life'' in Rembrandt's painting, and what Anderson says about Rembrandt is just as true when directed toward Anderson himself, whose finest tales do evoke a ''beyondness,'' exactly through the mechanism of suspension. In order to suspend an experience, the artist must create a perspective, a distance that the raw experience itself does not possess, and paradoxically the distance achieved does not in any way involve a cheap skipping beyond the actual; rather, it first enfolds ''all life'' on its way to beyondness. Anderson's mystic sphere never excludes; it always includes. There indeed exists an awareness of a presence ''glistening and clear . . . beautiful and strange,'' as Anderson puts it in *A Story Teller's Story* (408), but in no sense is ''wholeness'' lost. Perhaps Anderson's comment about his favorite French writer, Balzac, also applies to his own accomplishment; Balzac, he says, ''made his readers feel the universality and wonder of his mind'' (*STS*, 360).

On page 47 of the Paris notebook Anderson fashions another expression—one of his most memorable—of his concept of beauty, and in so doing provides another insight into how his art moves ''beyond life'' by embracing ''all of it'': ''One does not receive the caress of beauty thro the intellect. It creeps upon you or flashes down on you like a stroke of lightning. There is the necessity of readjustment, of rebuilding something within. Every new and beautiful thing seen destroys while it heals. You are a tender hurt, shattered thing emerging from the womb of some great mother. Silence and solitude the sweet, the golden thing. Long after perhaps we shall speak to each other.''

James Schevill, commenting on this passage, declares that

Anderson meant his disavowal of intellect to apply only to the first stage of the esthetic experience; in a second stage of discrimination, Anderson would enforce intellectually his credo of "simplicity, directness, wholeness." "If the first impulse to appreciate art was through the emotions," says Schevill, "one could differentiate between good and bad creative works only by means of the intellect" (140). Anderson apparently refers to this intellectual stage in the line, "Long after perhaps we shall speak to each other."

Schevill's interpretation, as correct as it may be, seems to me to have the effect of diverting Anderson's statement and rendering it inapplicable. Involved is the question of whether Anderson in his own art aims primarily at the heart or the head, and the subject cannot be dismissed by a bland *both/and*.

The best of Anderson's short stories, like the artworks he was observing in Paris, either creep up or flash down on the reader, and they offer little satisfaction to the intellect. Take, for instance (*STS*, Bk. III, N. VII), the episode of the "dark field": the two lovers caught by the woman's brothers, the crude scuffling and slashing and ludicrous running, the morose wedding. This inserted short story, although abbreviated, is comparable in mood and even in quality to the *Winesburg* tales. After reading it one is left with no logical explanation of what it has meant or where it has led; yet something esthetic and human has happened. Anderson has caught and held a fragment of life long enough for it to rise above itself; a human being has met pain and made a gesture; the reader has suffered and survived. One senses unmistakably that something has shattered and must now, after the reading, be repaired, and it seems to me Anderson is talking about precisely this in Paris Notebook, 1921. His conception of creating beauty is to freeze destruction long enough for it to be recognized as such, and the implication is that by facing the worst, one transcends it. In the godly, ghostly silence that follows a catastrophe, the reader stands quite firm and tall, staring down at what has been destroyed and thus knowing what about life is most valuable: an intuitive distance is built into the very act of confrontation. This experience, Anderson feels, cannot be received by the intellect.

The beauty Anderson saw around him in France affected him in exactly the same way he wished his tales to affect his readers, and his evaluations of Rembrandt or Sainte-Chapelle or Chartres make even more sense as evaluations of Anderson. He did de-emphasize the value of intellect in the esthetic experience; there is no getting around it. No one denies the possibility of genuine intellectual beauty, but Anderson's sensibilities were simply not attuned to either receive or dispense this type of beauty. When he tried to make his work intellectual, thesis-directed, it usually collapsed into the drab and mediocre, as many critics have pointed out, but when he trapped that emotional caress, lightning struck.

Several French critics have noted the centrality of "fancy," of imagination, as a theme in *A Story Teller's Story*, and they have attempted to define its specific nature.

Freudian Régis Michaud, for example, dwells on the episode which Anderson says marked the point at which his "own imaginative life began to take form" (*STS*, 94). Daydreaming in a hayloft, the child Anderson invents a fictional father. Beginning here, says Michaud in 1926, "for a long time now he has dreamed and imagined. It is his true, his only way of living."[13] Michaud goes further and claims "imagination" as Anderson's "ruling faculty" and "evocation by dream" as its regular form. "Who can speak here of realism?" asks Michaud. "Anderson . . . declares that only what has been imagined can be true."[14]

It must be noted here that Michaud's direction, predictable

for a Freudian, leads inevitably away from the real Anderson, for in *A Story Teller's Story* imagined *probable* scenes far outnumber the dream fantasies; most of his tales, though indeed created by fancy, are anchored in everyday waking fact.

Charles Cestre steers more safely when he observes that "the secret of Anderson's genius" is that his imagination "nourishes the 'données' of experience." [15] In the Chartres section of the autobiography Anderson depicts just such a *donnée*. This is the episode, already referred to, in which Anderson watched a man with his two women, one American and one French; the man "was flirting" with the Frenchwoman; the American was trying not to notice. Then, "the three of them just suddenly came out of the church together and walked away together in silence. That was all. All tales presented themselves to the fancy in just that way. There was a suggestion, a hint given. In a crowd of faces in a crowded street one face suddenly jumped out. It had a tale to tell, was crying its tale to the street but at best one got only a fragment of it" (402).

André Berge, in a 1928 review of *A Story Teller's Story*, was fascinated by Anderson's tendency to occupy himself, as he does here, even in his own autobiography, with the lives of others.[16] The typical French autobiographer, says Berge, would have evoked every possible memory of his past, would have analyzed every nuance of his own personality, "whereas Anderson's memories, drunk with independence, are on the verge of forgetting that they relate to a central narrator. An innate instinct for storytelling causes him to attribute more reality to other people than to himself. And what holds the largest place in his book is not the part of their existence that he has actually known, but rather that part that he has imagined." [17]

This imaginative living outside self in the lives of others

recurs as a motif throughout the autobiography, but it receives its strongest expression as a moral value in the story of Alonzo Berners (Bk. II, Ns. IX–XIII). Anderson is amazed by Berners' ability to attract other men simply by sitting quietly and listening. "His mind seemed always to follow the minds of the others" (250). Anderson begins to sense a unique wisdom in this man who appears to "have no life of his own": "Did most men and women remain children and was Alonzo Berners grown up? Was it grown up to come to the realization that oneself did not matter, that nothing mattered but a kind of consciousness of the wonder of life outside oneself?"

Association with Berners ultimately resulted in an almost religious conversion to the outward impulse. In one of the book's most powerful scenes, Anderson leaves Berners' house at night, and, standing in a dirt street, overcome by a need to worship, he kneels: "There was no God in the sky, no God in myself, no conviction in myself that I had the power to believe in a God, and so I merely knelt in the dust in the silence and no words came to my lips" (270). Kneeling he hears a child cry in a nearby house, and his fancy plays with the similarity between himself and "the wise men of old times who were reputed to have come to worship at the feet of another crying babe in an obscure place. How grand! The wise men of an older time had followed a star to a cowshed. Was I becoming wise? Smiling at myself and with also a kind of contempt of myself and my own sentimentality I half decided I would try to devote myself to something, give my life a purpose. 'Why not to another effort at the re-discovery of man by man?'" (271).

This existential decision obviously took effect, for Anderson soon incorporated it into his writing, into the creative process itself. A few pages later Anderson describes a fervent walk in the streets: "The walls of the houses are brushed away by the force of the imagination and one sees and feels all of the life within. What a universal giving away of secrets! Everything is felt; everything known. Physical life within one's own body comes to an end of consciousness. The life outside is all, everything. Now for the pen or the pencil and paper and I shall make you feel this thing I now feel" (290).

The euphoria of escape from self-consciousness so sweeps over Anderson's creative imagination that he can earnestly say, like Berners, "In myself I have no existence. Now I exist only in these others" (291). This mood always accompanied him when his writing was going well, and it became one of the most treasured gifts of the "fancy" because it was plainly the closest he could come to absorption into God.

And further, in *A Story Teller's Story* Anderson's dedication to love of other men tended at all points to intertwine with his love of beauty. Notice, for instance, the relationship between Rosenfeld and Anderson at Chartres: "My friend sat in silence. He had got hold of Huysmann's 'Cathedral' and was reading. Now and then he put the book down and sat for a long time in silence looking at the gray lovely old building in that gray light. It was one of the best moments of my own life. I felt free and glad. Did the friend who was with me love me? It was sure I loved him. How good his silent presence" (401). It is as if a mutual awareness of beauty were one of those strong "invisable cords," as he phrases it in his notebook (57), which bind individuals in a community of love. The notebook records a similar moment when beauty and community merge. In his Paris hotel, Anderson at three in the morning hears a nightingale suddenly begin "singing madly." As shutters open, Anderson knows that the entire neighborhood is listening to "the clear lovely notes. . . . The lovely bird had united all of us. For ten minutes all in the street listened carried out of our self by the sweet song of the bird" (32).

The idea here resembles that of Judge Turner in *A Story Tel-ler's Story*. Turner had instilled in the young Anderson a dream of the perfect relationship between two people: "We would live, I dreamed, each his own life, each gathering what beauty might be possible from the great outer world and bringing it as a prize to the other. There would be this man I loved and of whom I asked nothing and toward whom my whole impulse would be forever just to give and give to the very top of my bent" (181).

All of this indicates clearly that Anderson's esthetic devotion has ultimately led him directly into actual life, not out; directly into community, not into solipsism. From the early simplistic escapism, expressed in Book I of *A Story Teller's Story* when he says, "The dream that never can become a fact in life can be-come a fact in fancy" (25), he has advanced to a stage where life and fancy need no longer live apart as belligerents; now they can collaborate as comrades. Anderson has not suc-cumbed to his father's dime-novel romanticism; as a mature artist his fancy, rather than fleeing the real, opens a door into the secret chambers of the real. Esthetically and personally he ties himself to actual people. Art has not served as buffer against the actual; it has further exposed the actual. This is the significance of Anderson's weaving the story of the pathetic love triangle into his adoration of Chartres Cathedral. As the slighted woman leans on the door crying, Anderson thinks, "Life went on then, ever in the same tragic comic sweet way. In the presence of the beautiful old church one was only more aware, all art could do no more than that—make people, like my friend and myself, more aware" (401).

During the search for something "to glisten and shine out-side the muddle of life" (408), Anderson had gradually come to see that the muddle itself, activated by imagination, could glisten and shine, and as part of this realization, he had developed a genuine gusto for every phase of the muddle. For instance, although in Europe he worshiped at such ideal repositories of beauty as the Louvre and Chartres, he also worshiped at cafés, on the streets, and by the river. I think it informative to note that in *A Story Teller's Story*, Book IV, Note VIII, just before the paean to Chartres, Anderson amalgamates and condenses street observations (recorded in PN, 41–44) into a scene of "little delightful mental notes" viewed from a Paris café, concentrating on the laughing uninhibited lovemaking of a boy and girl and on the staunch virility of the cart horses (388). Fancy welcomes daily facts.

And in the notebook, when one reads Anderson's lists of the objects that, he feels, evince the caress of beauty, one is struck by the democracy of the juxtapositions. Fieldworkers and Fontainebleau, seamstresses and Sainte-Chapelle, dirty shirts and the Louvre sit side by side in complete harmony (46). Anderson as a modern artist joins hands with old masters and present-day plain citizens. As he says a few pages after these lists, "It is only the moderns and the old old men of the middle ages who seem to approach life and beauty" (50).

Anderson, then, arrives not at a choice between fact and fancy, as the early pages of *A Story Teller's Story* suggest he might, but at a marriage of the two, at a love of fact clarified and illuminated by fancy. As Léon-Gabriel Gros says about the autobiography: "Anderson unites a strange dream-like power with the most down-to-earth—carnal would be more accurate—sense of low realities, and because of this we find here a personality which, depending on whether one considers this or that aspect, brings to mind sometimes Rilke and at other times Istrati."[18] At his best Anderson fuses dreaminess and earthiness into a single mature look at the essentials of being human.

One noteworthy aspect of this maturity is a renewed appreciation of America. Anderson had "looked abroad" in a push toward perspective; he had assimilated what Europe had to offer him, and he was ready to go home. Toward the end of the Chartres episode in *A Story Teller's Story*, Anderson reflects about his own and Rosenfeld's futures: "We would both soon be going back to America to our separate places there. We wanted to go, wanted to take our chances of getting what we could out of our own lives in our own places. We did not want to spend our lives living in the past, dreaming over the dead past of a Europe from which we were separated by a wide ocean" (407). Anderson begins to discern that "For all one might say about American life it had been good to me" (404). In Paris Notebook, 1921 Anderson reaches similar conclusions. Walking in the Palais Royal, he and Rosenfeld discuss the problem: "We talked of America, both agreeing that while American cities were all comparatively ugly nothing would tempt us to come away to live permanently in a European city" (36). And in the notebook he begins to jot down positive American traits that he could not find in Europeans: sensitivity (24), intellectual flexibility (45), generosity (50).

European tradition had infused into Anderson a new awareness of the possibilities of art, but those possibilities must realize themselves in the midst of everything American. As he says in *A Story Teller's Story*:

I was happiest when I was in the mood into which I had fallen on the day when I sat before the cathedral—that is to say, when I sat rolling over and over the little colored stones I had managed to gather up. The man with the two women had just dropped another into my hands. How full my hands were! How many flashes of beauty had come to me out of American life.

It was up to me to carve the stones, to make them more beautiful if I could. . . . I had sought teachers and had found a few. (409)

But the best commentary on the final meaning of the auto-biography, and on what lasting effect Anderson's experience with France had on his art, comes from Anderson in a letter he wrote to Rosenfeld shortly after their return from Europe in 1921:

Now you understand Paul something in me. There is acceptance. . . . I take these little ugly factory towns, these sprawling cities into something. I wish it would not sound silly to say I pour a dream over it, consciously, intentionally, for a purpose. I want to write beau-tifully, create beautifully, not outside but in this thing in which I am born, in this place where in the midst of ugly towns, cities, Fords, moving pictures, I have always lived, must always live. I do not want, Paul, even those old monks at Chartres, building their cathedral, to be at bottom any purer than myself. . . .

There are men, like Jones of the Chicago Post, who, having no doubt at some time heard me say something derogative to smart men and smartness have got the idea fixed in their heads that I am without respect for old things, old beauty. . . . I just don't want any of you fellows who are real, who love beauty and who understand more than I ever will, to be fooled by my crudeness or to be led to believe that I am not, in my own way, trying to live in the old tradition of the artists. (Fall, 1921)

Anderson very probably had this challenge, this "trying," in mind when he wrote the Epilogue to *A Story Teller's Story*. Here another European art object becomes emblematic, in the same way Chartres had been, of what Rex Burbank calls "imaginative fulfillment in love and art, the symbol of a whole people welded together for the creation of beauty"[19]—the kind of esthetic and human devotion that Anderson strove to carry to his experience of America.

Just before leaving Anderson's room, a troubled and money-corrupted American writer has flung down Anderson's be-loved copy of *The Tales of Balzac*. Anderson closes his auto-biography with these lines: "The soft brown leather back is uninjured and now again, in fancy, the name of the author is staring at me. The name is stamped on the back of the book in letters of gold.

"From the floor of my room the name Balzac is grinning ironically up into my own American face" (442).

Notes

CHAPTER 1

1. Newberry Library (Chicago), Special Collections. Unless otherwise indicated, all quoted letters are manuscripts in this collection; they will henceforth be identified by date in the text. At Newberry all letters *from* Anderson are filed under "Outgoing," *to* Anderson under "Incoming."

2. Ray Lewis White (ed.), *Sherwood Anderson's Memoirs* (Chapel Hill: University of North Carolina Press, 1969), 361–63.

3. In a personal letter to Michael Fanning, August 7, 1974.

4. Edmund Wilson, "Paul Rosenfeld: Three Phases," in Jerome Mellquist and Lucie Wiese (eds.), *Paul Rosenfeld: Voyager in the Arts* (New York: Creative Age Press, 1948), 6–7.

5. James Schevill, *Sherwood Anderson: His Life and Work* (Denver: University of Denver Press, 1951), 135.

6. Irving Howe, *Sherwood Anderson* (Stanford University Press, 1966), 132.

7. Harry Hansen, *Midwest Portraits* (New York: Harcourt, 1923), 168.

8. Lewis Galantière, "French Reminiscence," *Story*, XIX (September–October, 1941), 64, 65.

9. Claudine Chonez, "Du Middle West à Greenwich Village: Avec Sherwood Anderson: Européen d'Amérique," *Les Nouvelles littéraires* (March 26, 1938), 6. "J'aime la vie sous toutes ses formes. Je pense qu'il faut toujours être *ready for her, open.*" All translations are mine.

10. Mellquist and Wiese (eds.), *Rosenfeld*, 4, 5.

11. *No Swank* (Philadelphia: Centaur Press, 1934), 9, 10.

12. Chonez, "Du Middle West."

13. Ernest Hemingway, *A Moveable Feast* (New York: Scribner's, 1964), 35.

14. Sylvia Beach, *Shakespeare and Company* (New York: Harcourt, Brace, 1959),

30–32. Unless otherwise indicated, succeeding quotations from Miss Beach are from these pages.

15. Gertrude Stein, *The Autobiography of Alice B. Toklas* (New York: Harcourt, Brace, 1933), 132.

16. Beach, *Shakespeare and Company*, 13.

17. Galantière, "French Reminiscence," 65, 66.

18. Rex Burbank, *Sherwood Anderson* (New York: Twayne, 1964), 121.

19. Galantière, "French Reminiscence," 66, 67.

CHAPTER 2

1. Probably Konrad Bercovici, a naturalized Roumanian-born American author who wrote primarily books of travel and local color. Bercovici was also in Paris when Anderson visited in 1927.

2. Cf. p. 1 of Gertrude Stein, *Portrait of Mabel Dodge at the Villa Curonia* (1912). Carl Van Vechten (ed.), *Selected Writings* (New York: Random House, 1946), 463–68.

3. Cf. p. 28, Gertrude Stein, *Tender Buttons* (New York: Claire Marie, 1914).

4. *Ibid.*, cf. p. 56.

5. Cf. Anderson's introduction to Gertrude Stein's *Geography and Plays* (1922), reprinted in Ray Lewis White (ed.), *Sherwood Anderson/Gertrude Stein* (Chapel Hill: University of North Carolina Press, 1972), 15. The sentence in the text is unfinished. Perhaps writing about Stein reminded Anderson that he should start his own creative work, for here begins the "writing-book" section of the notebook.

6. Possibly George Borrow (1803–81), writer of exuberant travel and adventure books; one of Anderson's favorite authors.

7. This paragraph accurately describes Anderson's situation at Fairhope, Alabama, on the east side of Mobile Bay, where he stayed from late February, 1920, to late May of that year.

8. The tale fragment that begins here may well be Anderson's earliest attempt to write "Death in the Woods," one of his finest stories. Cf. William Miller's edition of "The Death in the Forest" in Ray Lewis White (ed.), *Tar: A Midwest Childhood, a Critical Text* (Chapel Hill: University of North Carolina Press, 1969), 231–36.

CHAPTER 3

1. Sherwood Anderson, *A Story Teller's Story* (New York: Viking, 1969), 185. All references are to this edition; page numbers will henceforth be indicated in parentheses.

2. Sisley Huddleston, *Paris Salons, Cafés, Studios* (New York: Blue Ribbon Books, 1928), 82.

3. Régis Michaud, *Le Roman Américain d'aujourd'hui* (Paris, 1926), 131. "voudrait, comme Ruskin et William Morris, nous aider à retrouver, à travers les distractions superficielles de la vie moderne, ce vieil amour du métier d'où notre culture est sortie.' "

4. Léon-Gabriel Gros, "Je suis un homme, par Sherwood Anderson (Kra),"

Cahiers du Sud (May), 319–20. "Les passages que l'on retiendra volontiers sont ceux . . . . où Sherwood, avec son apparente bonhomie fait entendre sa voix dans ce requisitoire contrela civilisation matérielle."

5. Claudine Chonez, "Du Middle-West à Greenwich Village: Avec Sherwood Anderson: Européen d'Amérique," *Les Nouvelles Littéraires* (March 26, 1938), 6. "Le livre du Story Teller's Story a eu du succès . . . parce que j'y defendais l'artisanat contre la standardisation. Mes compatriotes adorent être critiqués."

6. Lewis Galantière, "*A Story Teller's Story*, par Sherwood Anderson," *Vient de paraître* (May, 1925), 262–63.

7. Michaud, *Le Roman*, 137. "N'oublions pas cette fuite. Nous la retrouverons dans ses livres. . . . C'est une phase de la conversion. . . . Le renouvellement incessant de l'existence est un des dogmes de son évangile. L'évasion, le déracinement subits sont dans ses romans, comme dans la vie des saints, la condition du perfectionnement moral et de la sanctification, l'accès à une vie nouvelle. Quitte tout et suis-mois," prononce la voix à laquelle ses heros s'abandonnent.

8. Michaud, *Le Roman*, 133. "Eh bien! la page blanche est la pour vous le révéler!"

9. "C'est probablement cette notion poétique et mallarméenne du papier vierge, plaque sensible où vivent les mots, qui a inspiré à Anderson un intérêt spécial pour les écrits surréalistes de Mme. Gertrude Stein."

10. Galantière, "A Story Teller's Story," "Nous savons que, tout comme un surréaliste, il s'éprit très jeune des mots, et que ce fut un besoin impérieux de jouer avec eux que le pousse à gribouiller dans sa petite chambre d'ouvrier, à Chicago."

11. "S'est mis dans l'écriture comme on se met dans le reliure, la gravure ou la dorure, par amour de la belle matière à manier."

12. James Schevill, *Sherwood Anderson: His Life and Work* (Denver: University of Denver Press, 1951), 140.

13. Michaud, *Le Roman*, 129. "il y a longtemps qu'il rève et qu'il imagine. C'est sa véritable, son unique façon de vivre."

14. *Ibid.*, 131. "faculté maîtresse," "l'évocation par le rêve"; "Qui parle ici de réalisme? Anderson . . . déclare que cela seul est vrai qui a été imaginé."

15. Charles Cestre, "Sherwood Anderson: A Story-Teller's Story," *Revue Anglo-Américaine* (December, 1925), 175–78. "le secret du génie d'Anderson," "nourrie les données de l'expérience."

16. André Berge, "Sherwood Anderson.—Un conteur se raconte: I. Mon père et moi (Kra)," *La Revue Nouvelle* (October), 171–72.

17. *Ibid.*, "tandis que les souvenirs d'Anderson, ivres d'indépendance, sont sur le point d'oublier qu'ils se rapportent à un narrateur central. Un instinct inné de conteur lui fait attribuer plus de réalité aux autres personnages qu'à lui-même. Et ce qui tient la plus grande place dans son livre, ce n'est pas la partie de leur existence qu'il a connue, mais bien celle qu'il a imaginée."

18. " Anderson unit à une étrange puissance de rêve le sens le plus terre à terre, charnel serait juste, des pauvres réalités, et de ce fait nous trouvons là un esprit qui, suivant qu'on le considère en tel ou tel de ses aspects, fait tantôt songer à Rilke et tantôt à Istrati."

19. Rex Burbank, *Sherwood Anderson* (New York: Twayne, 1964), 122.

Index